Native Peoples of North America

Diversity and development

Susan Edmonds

Copleston High School

CAMBRIDGE
UNIVERSITY PRESS

For Pete and my parents, Reg and Mary

PUBLISHED BY THE PRESS SYNDICATE OF THE UNIVERSITY OF CAMBRIDGE
The Pitt Building, Trumpington Street, Cambridge, United Kingdom

CAMBRIDGE UNIVERSITY PRESS
The Edinburgh Building, Cambridge CB2 2RU, UK
40 West 20th Street, New York, NY 10011–4211, USA
10 Stamford Road, Oakleigh, VIC 3166, Australia
Ruiz de Alarcón 13, 28014 Madrid, Spain
Dock House, The Waterfront, Cape Town 8001, South Africa

http://www.cambridge.org

First published 1993
Fifth printing 2001

Printed in the United Kingdom at the University Press, Cambridge

A catalogue record for this book is available from the British Library

Library of Congress Cataloguing in Publication data
Edmonds, Susan
Native peoples of North America / diversity and development /
Susan Edmonds.
        p.   cm. – (Cambridge history programme. Key stage 3)
Includes index.
ISBN 0 521 42846 7 (hb)
1. Indians of North America – History.   2. Indians of North
America – Government relations.   3. Indians of North America – Social
conditions.   I. Title.   II. Series.
E77.E26   1993
970.004'97 – dc 20   93-2181   CIP

Notice to teachers
Many of the sources used in this book
have been adapted or abridged from the original.

ISBN 0 521 42846 7

Illustrations by Adrian Day, Jeff Edwards, Donald Harley and Peter Kent
Maps by Martin Sanders
Picture research by Callie Kendall

Contents

Old wounds in a new world

A shocking defeat

1876 was an important year for the white people of the United States of America — it was the 100th anniversary of their country's birth. The celebrations in Washington were ruined, however, by news from the American West. The 7th Cavalry, led by a famous general, George Custer, had been defeated by a huge band of Indian warriors. Custer and all the men in his detachment had been wiped out on the banks of the Little Bighorn River.

Victory for the Sioux?

The Battle of the Little Bighorn was the climax of nearly 400 years of conflict between white Americans and Indians. But the killing of Custer and his men stood out from the other battles because, for once, the Indians were the winners and not the victims. It was, however, a victory which had far-reaching consequences for the Indians and the Sioux in particular, as you will discover in a later unit.

Source A

A painting of the Battle of the Little Bighorn by the Sioux Indian, Kicking Bear, who was a warrior at the battle in 1876. This is the only known eyewitness painting. It shows the scene at the end of the battle. Sitting Bull, the Sioux chief, is amongst the men standing near the centre; Custer lies dead to the left of centre. It gives us an idea of the clothes worn and weapons used.

- *What information can we not get from Kicking Bear's painting?*

- *How reliable are the pictures of the Battle of the Little Bighorn?*

What happened at Little Bighorn?

There were no survivors on the US cavalry side and the Indians who fought were unwilling to talk about the details of the battle. Despite this lack of evidence, many artists have tried to depict this important moment in American history and both sides produced pictures to show how Custer and his men died.

- Why do you think that the battle was such a popular subject in the late nineteenth century?

Source B

A painting of the Battle of the Little Bighorn by Edgar Paxson, 1899. This picture was painted after ten years of detailed research into the battle. Paxson visited the site, looked at earlier pictures and read accounts of the battle. He was anxious that it should be a fair representation of the battle, while also being a fine piece of art that would further his reputation. Custer is seen standing in the centre of the picture.

- *What problems would Paxson have found in researching the evidence for his picture?*

- *What can we learn from these images about the different people who fought for America?*

A New World?

The continent of America is sometimes called the 'New World'. This name was used by the Europeans who discovered it at the end of the fifteenth century. Until then, they did not know that this great land mass even existed and yet America had been inhabited for thousands of years. To the people who already lived there — the native peoples of North America — the land was not new; it was their ancient home.

Discovery!

When Europeans first came to America they discovered not only a continent but also an unknown race of people. These people came to be called Indians — a strange name for people living in America, thousands of miles from India!

The name resulted from the famous mistake of the explorer, Christopher Columbus. He set sail from Spain in 1492. Unaware of the existence of America, he believed that his ships had landed at the Spice Islands near India. He named the islands the Indies and their people the Indians. He never did find out that they were in fact the Caribbean islands off the coast of the unknown continent, America.

From the fury and chaos of the Civil W
...to the final earth-shaking charge at I

CINERAMA presents
ROBERT SHAW as
CUSTER
OF THE
WEST

in all the sweep
and spectacle of CINERAMA

RY URE
FREY HUNTER, TY HARDIN, KIERON MOORE, LAWRENCE TIERN
d and Conducted by BERNARDO SEGÁLL. Released through CINERAMA INTERNATIONAL RE

WORLD PREMIERE
URSDAY 9th NOVEMBER   CAS

Source C

Christopher Columbus wrote about his new discovery and the Indians he met:

'So peaceful are these people that I swear there is not in the world a better nation. They love their neighbours as themselves, and their words are always gentle and accompanied with a smile; and though it is true that they are naked, their manners are praiseworthy.'

Christopher Columbus, letter to the King of Spain, 1492

Source D

Woodcut from a letter written by Christopher Columbus in 1492. It shows the Europeans trying to trade with the native Carib Indians.

- *How has the artist shown the Indians?*

Images of Indians

Does the impression created by Sources A and B match the idea of Indians that many of us may have in our minds? Where are the feathers and face paint? Where are the bows and arrows or the horses and wigwams?

Perhaps we should first ask ourselves where our idea of Indians comes from. Indian people have been shown all over the world on television and cinema screens as fierce warriors fighting cowboys and the white American settlers. But we should question this Hollywood image, and the drawing

- What were Columbus' first impressions of the Indians he met?

the glory days of the 7th Cavalry Big Horn!

...ERT RYAN as Mulligan   Written by BERNARD GORDON and JULIAN HALEVY.   Directed by ROBERT SIODMAK.
...ney Pictures, Inc. Film   Photographed in SUPER TECHNIRAMA® TECHNICOLOR®

CINERAMA THEATRE   OLD COMPTON ST. W.1.   GER 6877

Source E

The Battle of Little Bighorn as shown on a Hollywood film poster, 1967.

from Christopher Columbus' letter is a good starting place. As you learn more about the Indians' history you can add to this picture and build up a more accurate understanding of the Indians and their culture.

A rich and varied past

In the first section of this book you will find out about the ancient ancestors of the Indians that Columbus met. Long before the Europeans came, in the late fifteenth century, Indians had developed a great variety of cultures. Individual tribes had particular types of home, various ways of getting food, their own languages, different ways of fighting and their own forms of religion.

Struggle for America

In his letter, Christopher Columbus went on to write: 'They [the Indians] should be made to work, farm and live like us.' This gives us some idea of the differences between the Europeans and the Indians and shows that, from the earliest contact, some Europeans believed that the Indians should change their way of life. Many Europeans who felt that their own culture was far better, described the Indians as savages. They therefore felt that it was in the interest of the Indians to learn about Christianity and the European way of life.

From the sixteenth century, the Indian story became one of a struggle to keep their land and traditions as more and more Europeans made their homes in America. Over the following centuries, treaties were made and battles were fought until the Indians were so weak that they could fight no more. The Sioux, whose history you will study in detail, fiercely resisted the Europeans. Their story, which represents the struggle of many of the other tribes, is told in the second and third sections of this book.

Indians today

Although the Indians were not successful in resisting the influence of the advancing Europeans, they were not completely wiped out; their story continues today. In the final section of the book we look at Indians who live a life that combines traditional Indian and modern American culture.

Source F

There are approximately 1 million Indians in America today. Although many of their traditions have been lost, they still keep their tribal loyalties and many feel themselves to be more Indian than American.

North America –

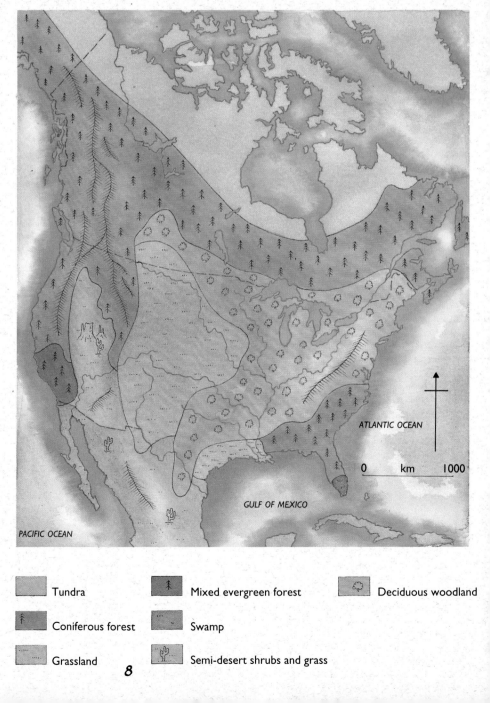

Ice Age to 1500 – Prehistory

A period of history before written evidence is known as prehistory. In North America there were no written records until the arrival of Europeans in about AD 1500. Writing was not a part of Indian culture. Their languages were spoken only.

The relief and land types of North America

The continent of North America has many landscapes and climates. The far north is too cold for most plants, while the south west is too hot and dry. In between, fertile and wooded lands are broken up by mountain ranges and dry grasslands.

At the time when people first arrived, between 20,000 BC and 10,000 BC, this land supported many animals. Some we would recognise: the elk, the moose, the deer. Others would have been a much stranger sight: the mammoth, the long-horned bison, the giant sloth. These were very large animals that later became extinct. This was the land that the ancient ancestors of the Indians made their home.

- Study the map and decide where you would have chosen to live.

ATLANTIC OCEAN

0   km   1000

GULF OF MEXICO

PACIFIC OCEAN

Tundra   Mixed evergreen forest   Deciduous woodland

Coniferous forest   Swamp

Grassland   Semi-desert shrubs and grass

the first people

The Ice Age: 26,000 BC to 12,000 BC

Ancestors of the Indians crossed from Asia to America during the Ice Age, almost 30,000 years ago. They may have come over a temporary land bridge which was formed as the sea shrank. Early inhabitants lived by hunting large animals with stone weapons.

12,000 BC to AD 100

By the first century AD, many areas of America were supporting villages of people, who lived not only by hunting but also by farming the land. The richest groups were in the desert areas of the south–west and the woodland areas of the east.

AD 100 to AD 1500

By about AD 1500, Indians had spread throughout the whole of America. Because of the variety of land and climate different groups of Indians developed many different ways of living.

Evidence

How can we find out about prehistoric times if there is no written evidence? Historians have to use clues that have been left behind in the ground. These are the clues of archaeology. They include objects like jewellery, weapons or pots which have not rotted away. There might also be the remains of buildings or bones. Many objects can be dated quite accurately by scientific methods.

To understand Indian history in the long period before 1500, we must fit these archaeological clues together.

Shell bead necklaces with stone and abalone shell pendants used by the Pomo tribe in California.

This Plains Indian man lived 1300 years ago in the Rocky Mountains. His body was placed in a cave in the foetal position which symbolised rebirth – the return of his spirit to the earth in human or animal form.

Cliff Palace, Mesa Verde. This cliff dwelling was the centre of a Colorado chiefdom over 900 years ago and from it we can learn much about the lives and customs of the Indians of the south-west.

These worn-out moccasins, which were preserved in the dry soil inside a cave in Utah, were patched up and finally discarded over 1500 years ago.

9

Across the land bridge

The faces of modern Indians look similar to those of some people from east Asia. This is because American Indians are descended from people of east Asian origin.

How and when did the early people come to North America?

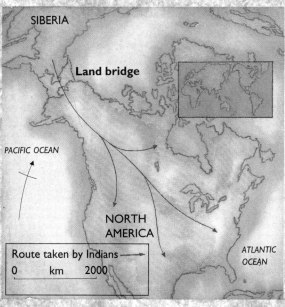

North America joined to Asia by the land bridge during the Great Ice Age.

SIBERIA

Land bridge

PACIFIC OCEAN

NORTH AMERICA

ATLANTIC OCEAN

Route taken by Indians
0   km   2000

Source A

A modern historian writes:

'During some periods, the land bridge was about 1,000 miles wide, and there is no reason to suppose that the people realised that they were crossing from one continent to another. Small groups of hunters probably crossed over many times following the animals that they hunted.'

William Hodge, *The First Americans*, 1981

- Why did people cross the land bridge?

When the ice melted at the end of the Ice Age, the people from Asia had already made their homes in the continent of America. As the sea level rose, they were cut off from the old world of Asia and Europe. This isolation lasted for thousands of years and meant that Indian culture developed in its own way without outside influence.

Nature's bridge

Many thousands of years ago, nature made a link between the lands of Asia and North America. During the last Ice Age (which ended about 12,000 years ago) so much of the world's water was frozen that the sea shrank. Where the sea had been shallow, such as in the Bering Strait (see map), there was dry land and people could walk across the temporary land bridge. This is probably the way that people first came to North America.

Source B - Clovis spear point

This stone was carved into a spear point in about 10,000 BC. It was found at a place called Clovis in New Mexico. These plentiful weapons provide the earliest evidence of people which is accepted by all archaeologists.

Looking at the evidence

A famous archaeologist called Dr Louis Leakey believes that people were in America thousands of years before the Clovis spear point was carved.

He found stones in California that seemed to have been carved by people over 65,000 years ago.

Other archaeologists do not agree with Dr Leakey. They say that the chipped stone tools he was using as evidence could have been shaped by nature rather than by people. They believe that the real date of the arrival of people in North America was much later.

Dean Snow put the environmental and archaeological evidence together in a table to work out when people could have arrived in America.

Source C

Date BC	Environmental evidence	Archaeological evidence
32,000		People not yet adapted to living in the extreme cold northern climates
30,000	Land bridge under water	
28,000		
26,000	Land bridge clear	A few human bones and tools found
24,000		
22,000	Ice blocks the area south of the landbridge –	
20,000	people cannot pass through	
18,000		
16,000		
14,000	Land bridge clear again – passage to America open	
12,000		
10,000	Ice Age ends – landbridge under water	Many spear points found throughout North America
8,000		

Dean Snow, *The American Indians — Their Archaeology and Prehistory*, 1976.

---

1 Why do you think that spear points are the most frequently found evidence of the earliest Indians?

2 Look at Source C to answer the following:

a At what dates would it have been possible to cross the land bridge?

b What is the earliest date that people could have arrived in North America?

c By what date could you say that people definitely lived in North America?

3 According to Source C, Dr Leakey's theory would not be possible. Why not?

4 How is it possible that historians can have such different views about the arrival date? (Think about the type and amount of evidence.)

From hunters to farmers

With the extinction of the large hunting animals and the development of better tools, the lives of the Indians changed. Many, including people of the South West desert area, had stopped living as hunters, had settled in villages and were growing their own crops by about 200 BC.

What evidence is there for a change in the way of life in the South West desert area?

Settling in villages

Look back at the map on page 8 and find the South West desert area. Towns like Pueblo Bonito provide impressive evidence of a new way of life in this part of America. The change from wandering hunters to settled villagers was gradual and must have taken many years. Villagers would have continued to hunt but probably only for smaller animals like rabbit and deer. As people became better at feeding themselves they had more time for art and leisure. Evidence for these changes can be found by looking at the archaeological clues.

A mysterious end

Although the people of Pueblo Bonito had developed a rich culture, it had largely disappeared by AD 1300. The most probable explanation is a combination of crop failure and invading enemy tribes. However, the traditions of the Indians of the South West desert region can be seen in the art and architecture of their direct descendants, the Pueblo Indians, who still occupy parts of the South West today.

Source B

A decorated pot, over 2,000 years old, which was probably used for storing food.

Source C

This spear point was found between the remains of a bison's ribs. It is about 12,000 years old.

Source D

This ball court in Arizona was used by Indians for playing games about 1,300 years ago.

Source A

Present-day remains of Pueblo Bonito, an ancient desert town. At its peak, in AD 1100, it had over 800 homes and 1,200 inhabitants.

Source E

These cultivated corn cobs, which were found in a cave, are about 5,000 years old.

---

1 Why do you think Pueblo Bonito was built in the shape it was?

2 Look at Sources A – E. Each one is an archaeological clue. Copy the table below. List each source chronologically (oldest first) and complete the table. The first one has been done for you.

3 In your own order of importance, list three achievements of the prehistoric Indians of the South West.

Source	Date	Clue	What does the clue tell us?
C	10,000 BC	Spearhead in bison rib	People hunted large animals using stone weapons

The mound builders

The country which we now call the USA is divided by archaeologists studying prehistory into two main areas: the South Western Desert and the East Woodland area. The groups of people in these regions lived in different sorts of environments but they had all achieved agricultural skills by about 1000 BC. In other ways, however, their lifestyles had developed quite differently.

What do we know about the prehistoric Indians of the East Woodlands?

Rituals of death

Look for the East Woodland area on the map on page 8. Just as Pueblo Bonito provides us with evidence of the way of life of the people who lived there, so the remains of the large mounds built by the East Woodland Indians tell us much about their society and culture.

In the East Woodland area, the prehistoric people spent a lot of time and effort on the rituals of death. They built large earth mounds for burying their dead, some of which rivalled the Great Pyramids of Egypt in size. Sometimes there was a temple on the summit of the mound, burning an eternal fire. Most mounds were a simple circular shape but some followed quite complicated patterns. The most extraordinary site is the 2,000-year-old Serpent Mound, which winds in and out like a snake on top of a hill in the modern state of Ohio.

Grave goods

High-quality jewellery, weapons and pots were often buried with the dead. Most objects had not suffered the wear and tear of everyday use and were in such good condition that many archaeologists believe that they were made specially for the dead. The production of such items encouraged the development of craft skills among these people and possibly encouraged trade between different communities.

Source A

A modern historian describes the burial tradition of this region about 2,000 years ago:

'At the centre of a mound, at ground level, were one or more tomb chambers made of carefully carpentered logs, containing up to three bodies richly provided with all kinds of grave goods. Above these chambers hundreds of thousands of basketfuls of specially selected and graded types of earth were piled up and tramped down. This must have required an enormous amount of work.'

Jon Manchip White, *Everyday Life of the American Indian*, 1979

Source B

Decorated conch shell from Spiro Mound which dates from between AD 1200 and AD 1500. It is thought to show a ceremonial dancer in the costume of an eagle.

- *What do you think this shell may have been used for?*

A modern artist's reconstruction of a Temple Mound village in Georgia.

Ordered societies

Until 1000 BC, all graves in this area had been quite similar. After that date, the graves started to vary from the very simple to the very elaborate. This suggests that society had become divided into classes, with the rich and powerful at the top and the poor at the bottom. When Europeans explored the South East in the sixteenth century they discovered societies with a great gulf between the rich and poor. Sometimes the king-like figure at the top was so important that he was carried everywhere and treated like a god.

Source D

The South East was one of the first areas to be explored by Europeans in the sixteenth century. Their written descriptions give historians an idea of how people may have lived in the late prehistoric period. A modern historian writes:

'Hernando De Soto [a Spaniard] visited the Creek Indians when he made his famous trip through the South East in 1540–42. He said that the Creeks had a well–organised political and social system. There were public ceremonies around the temple platforms and ball games were played in the towns. Large towns dominated their surrounding countryside.'

Dean Snow, *The American Indians — Their Archaeology and Prehistory*, 1976

• Why do you think that the early explorers might have been surprised to see large towns in America?

---

1 a Describe the dancer's costume in Source B.
b What does Source B tell us about South Eastern religion?

2 The prehistoric period ended in about AD 1500. How useful are the observations of Hernando De Soto in 1540–42 (Source D) for telling us about prehistoric society?

3 Sources A and C are modern reconstructions of the past.

a What kind of archaeological finds would you expect Source A to be based on?
b What kind of archaeological finds would you expect Source C to be based on?
c Could the details of Source C be based on any other types of evidence, e.g. written or picture evidence? Explain fully.

4 'The graves of the dead help us to understand how they lived.' Do you agree with this statement? Give reasons for your answer.

Indians across America

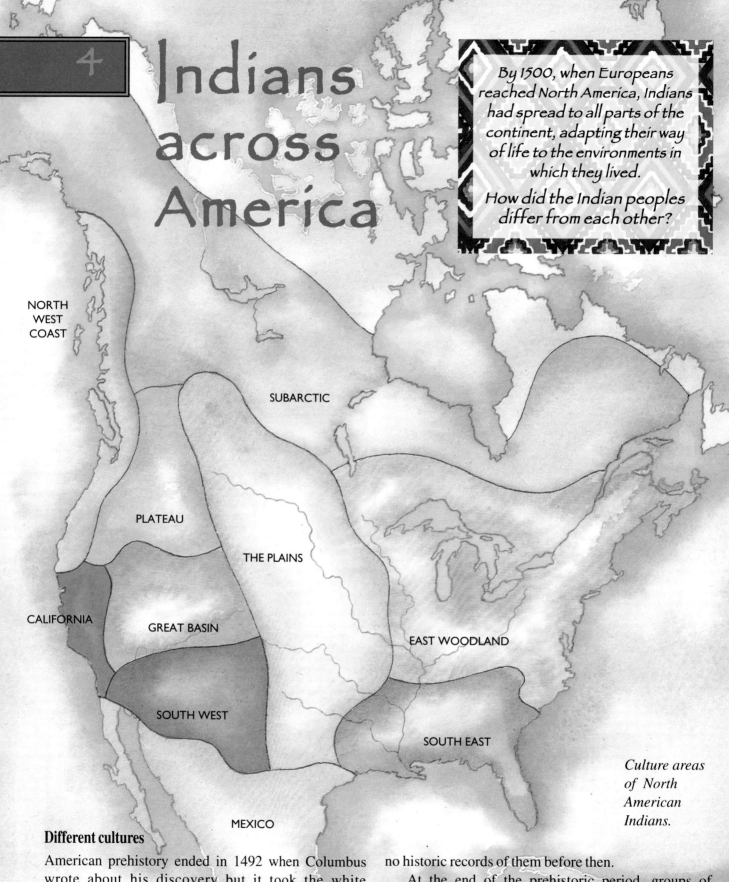

By 1500, when Europeans reached North America, Indians had spread to all parts of the continent, adapting their way of life to the environments in which they lived.

How did the Indian peoples differ from each other?

NORTH WEST COAST

SUBARCTIC

PLATEAU

THE PLAINS

CALIFORNIA

GREAT BASIN

EAST WOODLAND

SOUTH WEST

SOUTH EAST

MEXICO

Culture areas of North American Indians.

Different cultures

American prehistory ended in 1492 when Columbus wrote about his discovery but it took the white Europeans over 300 years to spread across North America, gradually meeting new groups of Indian people. Indians of the remote western lands did not meet white people until the nineteenth century and so we have no historic records of them before then.

At the end of the prehistoric period, groups of Indians with similar lifestyles can be divided into ten different areas, as shown on the map. These are called culture areas.

Environment and food

The table below describes the natural vegetation of each area and how the Indians used it for supplying their food.

Culture area	Vegetation	Food sources
Arctic (Inuit)	Snow covered — no trees	Hunted seals, whales and caribou
Subarctic	Coniferous forest (e.g. pine and fir trees)	Fished and hunted animals like moose and caribou
East Woodland	Woodland	Hunted and fished. Collected wild plants and grew crops like corn and beans
South East	Woodland	Hunted, fished and grew some crops
The Plains	Dry grassland	Hunted buffalo and collected wild plants
Great Basin and South West	Desert, semi-desert and grassland	Hunted desert animals and gathered wild plants. Farmed in South West
North West Coast and Plateau	Coniferous forest	Hunted many different animals and fished
California	Mixed forest	Collected wild plants. Fished and hunted

Indian homes

Different landscapes and climates required different types of home. As early Europeans moved from one area to another, they would have seen homes of varying shapes made from different building materials.

- Which home do you think would be the easiest to build?

Arctic

Eskimo — or Inuit — Indians lived in igloos during the coldest winter months when the ground was covered by deep snow.

North West

Homes were made from wood. Outside, they erected tall, colourfully painted, totem poles. These poles told a magical story of the family's history.

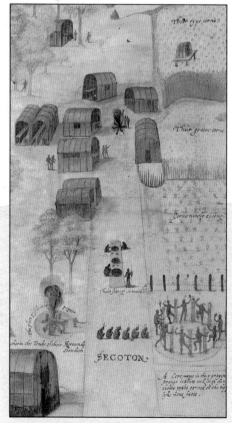

Source A

Painting of Secota, an East Woodland village, painted by John White in the sixteenth century. These tall, wooden-framed houses were called 'wigwams'. They were also common in the South East. The walls and roofs were covered with tightly woven reed mats or bark.

- *What evidence of farming is there? What do you think the people are doing in the centre and bottom of the picture?*

18

Great Basin and South West

These homes, built in the driest areas, were made from bundles of dried grass and brushwood. They were called 'wickieups'. Further east the Pueblo Indians used rich baked clay to build strong square houses.

The Plains and Subarctic

In some areas, lodges were made from earth, branches and grass. Tepees made from animal skins were constructed by the Plains Indians while those living in the Subarctic used tree bark.

1 On an outline map of North America:

a mark on the culture areas.

b make up symbols for the different types of vegetation and the different methods used for getting food (hunting, fishing, gathering wild plants and farming). Mark these on the map.

c draw in the types of housing for as many areas as possible. Don't forget to give your map a key.

2 In your own words, explain how Indians of the Arctic, the North West and the South West adapted to their environment.

3 Write down any reasons you can think of to explain why the tribes of North America were so different from each other.

1500 – 1860 Indian tribes

In AD 1500, there were approximately 1 million Indians living in North America. They lived in over 600 tribes which contained from 300 to 30,000 people, with the larger tribes divided up into smaller bands. Each tribe had its own way of life and the differences between them can be seen in the way they hunted and farmed, how they brought up their children and built their homes, and in the languages they spoke. The Sioux were one of the largest groups of Indians and were subdivided into seven tribes.

Indian tribes of North America

Many tribes did not stay in just one place. The Sioux, for example, did not originally live on the Plains but in the East Woodland area, where they lived in wooden villages, fishing and growing crops. Very rarely did they venture on to the Plains to hunt buffalo. But in the eighteenth century their way of life was threatened by white traders who gave guns to the Ojibwa tribe, the deadly enemies of the Sioux. To avoid a war and to find better hunting lands to support their growing population, the Sioux abandoned their villages in Minnesota and by 1750, their tepee camps were spread out from the Mississippi River to the Black Hills of South Dakota.

You can find many tribal names on maps of the USA— Kansas, Ohio and Michigan are examples. The name Sioux was given to them by the Ojibwa: it meant rattlesnake or adder. The Sioux called themselves Dakota, which means friends or allies; the present-day Plains states of North and South Dakota, where they came to live, are named after them.

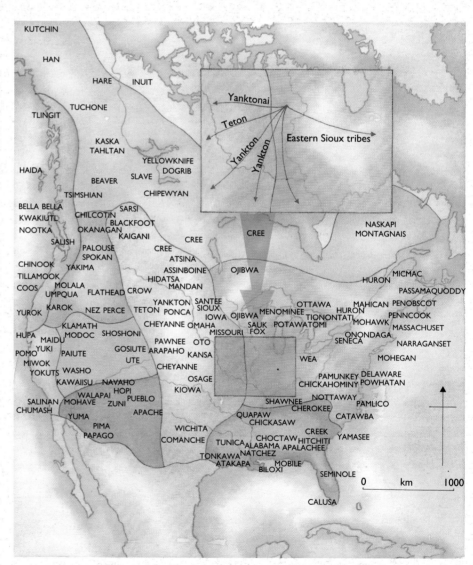

This map does not show the names of all the Indian tribes but gives an impression of the great number of different groups of native people living in North America.

• Look at the map on page 16 to identify the culture areas of these Indian tribes.

land of the Indian tribes

Tribal Culture of the Sioux

Government

The Sioux people were split up into smaller tribes, governed by chiefs who made decisions about such things as moving camp and making war. The chiefs relied on the advice of other senior men in their group.

Homes

The Sioux moved their camps to follow the buffalo herds. They lived in tepees made of buffalo skin which the women transported when the group moved camp.

Food

The Sioux relied on the buffalo for their food. Hunting was dangerous but the buffalo provided the raw materials for many everyday needs. The women collected wild plants and berries but the Sioux did not farm on the Plains.

Religion

According to the Sioux, all things and all creatures possessed a spirit. They worshipped these spirits and the Great Spirit which controlled all things and performed many dances and rituals to please them.

War

Bravery in battle was very highly respected among the Sioux. They did not generally fight long wars, making short raids on enemy tribes for horses or revenge but they rarely fought over land. The most frequently used weapons were bows and arrows, spears and war clubs.

Evidence

Increased contact with white Europeans during this period means that there is a wide range of written and picture evidence about the Plains Indians. Nineteenth-century explorers wrote down, and sometimes painted, what they saw. White settlers, soldiers and newspaper journalists also had their stories of the Plains and the Sioux, in particular.

Many Indian artefacts such as this Sioux hair ornament made with quills and eagle feathers became collectors items for nineteenth-century white travellers.

> 'Every part of this earth is sacred to my people. We are part of the earth and it is part of us. We know that the white man does not understand our ways. The earth is not his brother, but his enemy, and when he has conquered it, he moves on.'

Chief Seattle made this speech in 1854. Previously the Sioux language had not been recorded but after this time the words of many chiefs were written down and these translations provide valuable evidence of the lives of Indians as seen through their own eyes.

> 'These men were thorough savages. Their religion, their superstitions and their prejudices were the same that had been handed down to them from the immemorial time. They fought with the same weapons that their fathers fought with, and wore the same rude garments of skin.'

Frances Parkman Jr., The Oregon Trail, 1849. This popular nineteenth-century book reveals a common attitude to Indians and helped to create an image of their way of life which persisted for hundreds of years.

Sioux Camp Scene by Alfred J. Miller. This painting presents another view of the Indian way of life as seen by a white traveller. How does it differ from the impression created by Frances Parkman Jr.?

5 The Sioux nation

There were many Sioux people. Their societies were carefully organised to make sure that the people were as well fed and as safe as possible.

How were the tribes of the Sioux organised?

Source A

A Sioux Indian council, *painted by Seth Eastman in 1849. Unlike many other Indian tribes, Sioux women played no direct part in governing the tribe.*

Tribal structure

According to the records of French colonists, there were 25,000 members of the Sioux tribes in the seventeenth century: this made them one of the largest of all Indian peoples. A group of this many people could not survive as one unit so they became divided into seven major tribes. The largest and most powerful of these seven, the Teton Sioux, was divided into a further seven sub-tribes. These sub-tribes were then divided into family-based hunting groups or bands. The seven major tribes did not fight against each other, but they were not close friends and they did not get together to fight their many common enemies.

Governing the Teton tribes

Each family hunting group, or band, was led by a respected senior man, called a chief. He tried to make sure that his band were well fed and safe from danger. Each sub-tribe of the Tetons also had a head chief. From these seven head chiefs a tribal council of the four most senior Tetons was chosen.

Decision-making was not the job of the chiefs alone. Each tribe had councils of men who met together to discuss and make decisions about war, hunting and moving camp. Their opinions were the basis of the chiefs' decisions.

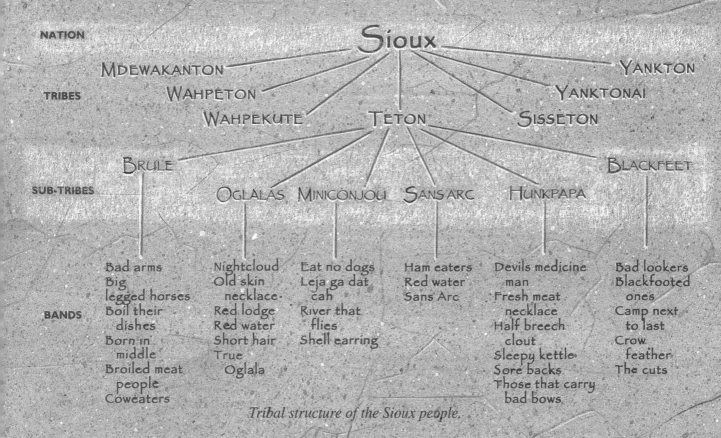

NATION	Sioux					
TRIBES	MDEWAKANTON				YANKTON	
	WAHPETON				YANKTONAI	
	WAHPEKUTE	TETON		SISSETON		
SUB-TRIBES	BRULE	OGLALAS	MINICONJOU	SANS ARC	HUNKPAPA	BLACKFEET
BANDS	Bad arms	Nightcloud	Eat no dogs	Ham eaters	Devils medicine	Bad lookers
	Big legged horses	Old skin necklace	Leja ga dat cah	Red water	man	Blackfooted ones
	Boil their dishes	Red lodge	River that flies	Sans Arc	Fresh meat necklace	Camp next to last
	Born in middle	Red water	Shell earring		Half breech clout	Crow feather
	Broiled meat people	Short hair			Sleepy kettle	The cuts
	Coweaters	True Oglala			Sore backs	
					Those that carry bad bows	

Tribal structure of the Sioux people.

The role of the chief

Any young man wanting to become a chief would have to work hard at developing his personal qualities. The most highly valued qualities were bravery, strength, generosity and wisdom. A good chief would have all of these and would probably also be from a wealthy family. He would need wealth to show his generosity. Once chosen as a chief, he encouraged others to develop these qualities by leading with his own example. He was given a special pipe and a brightly coloured shirt that was fringed with human hair which represented the people of his tribe.

Source B
George Catlin, one of the early European explorers of the Plains, wrote:

'The chief had no control over the life or freedom of his people, nor no other power whatever, except influence. He gains influence by his good example and bravery in war. All wars are decided upon by the chiefs and advisors in council. After their decision, the chief leads, his pipe is sent through the tribe and every man who agrees to go to war, breathes in the smoke. At the end of the fighting, the two parties are often brought together by a flag of truce, where the chiefs sit in Treaty, smoking through the pipe of peace.'

George Catlin, *Manners, Customs and Conditions of the North American Indians*, 1832–1839

- What qualities do we look for in a leader today?

1 Why was the Sioux nation divided into so many groups?

2 'The chief had total power over his tribe.' Do you agree with this statement? What evidence can you find to back up your answer?

3 Using all the information in this unit, explain the qualities needed by a chief and the different jobs he performed.

4 Imagine that a tribe wants a new chief. A group of Indians meet together to discuss the sort of person they want. Using information from this unit, write a script of their conversation.

Who can tell us about the Sioux?

Historical evidence is available to us both from the people who were present during the events — primary evidence — and from historians who have studied and written about them since — secondary evidence.

What sort of evidence can you use to find out about the Sioux?

The eyewitnesses

Different sorts of people witnessed the lifestyle of the Sioux Indians, particularly in the nineteenth century. These people can be divided into two groups: the Sioux Indians themselves and their white visitors. Both have left us a variety of types of primary evidence.

Evidence from the Sioux

A good starting place for investigation is to look at the artefacts. An artefact is an object produced by human workmanship. The Sioux pipe bowl in Source A tells us something about Sioux craftsmanship. We can see that the Sioux were skilled in the art of stone carving. We can also guess that they smoked but what else does it tell us? How can we find out more about the purpose of this beautifully carved object?

Luckily the sources of Indian evidence increased a great deal during the nineteenth century. Stories, conversations and speeches were translated and written down by visitors. These give us a chance to hear the thoughts of the Indians in their own words. Look at Source B carefully to find out more about the pipe.

Source B

Some words of the Sioux Indian, Chased-by-Bears, were written down in the nineteenth century:

'Before talking of holy things, we prepare ourselves by offerings. One will fill his pipe and hand it to the other who will light it and offer it to the sky and earth. They will smoke together and then they will be ready to talk.'

Frances Densmore, *Teton Sioux Music*, 1918

• What does this source tell you about the use of the Sioux pipe?

Source A

Sioux pipe end made out of a rare stone called catlinite. It was fitted onto a long hollow stem.

Evidence from white visitors

The central Plains were still a mystery to white Americans at the end of the eighteenth century. Stories of fantastic animals and landscapes were plentiful. The only white people who had seen it were the fur trappers and traders who reported little of what they saw. But in the first four decades of the nineteenth century some white Americans and Europeans set out to explore the American West. Some visitors were profit-seeking traders, others were armed soldiers, some were ordinary people looking for a new home.

In 1832, George Catlin, an artist from Philadelphia, decided to make the Indians of the West his life's work. He travelled for thousands of miles making detailed paintings and written records of what he saw. Artists and writers like George Catlin were the first to show the Plains Indians to the world and, fortunately, they recorded life on the Plains before it was greatly changed by contact with white America.

Source C

Red Pipestone Quarry painted by George Catlin in the 1830s. This is the site where the Sioux mined the stone for making their sacred pipes.

- *Why do you think the stone was called 'catlinite'?*

The history tellers

Modern historians tell us about the lives of the Sioux. They have spent time carefully studying the evidence. They use it to make their own interpretation of Sioux history. We can use their interpretations to find out more about the Sioux pipe.

Source D

'All the Sioux considered the pipestone quarry a holy place and came to it often to mine the special stone they used to make sacred pipes. At this holy place, Sioux people left offerings and held ceremonies to ask the Great Spirit's permission to dig for pipestone. Then they quarried stone and carved pipes for use in daily worship or special ceremonies.'

Herbert Hoover, *The Yankton Sioux*, 1988

---

1 Using Sources A to D, write down what you have discovered about the Sioux pipe.

2 Which source did you find most useful? Explain why.

3 a Using all the information on these pages, write a list of all the different sources of information on the Sioux Indians that you could use for research. Can you think of any that are not mentioned here?

b Put a 'P' by all those that are primary evidence and an 'S' beside all those that are secondary evidence.

Horses on the Plains

Although there had been horses in America at the time of the Ice Age, they became extinct soon after the ice had melted. They reappeared on the continent when the Spanish brought them over from Europe in the sixteenth century.

What happened when horses were introduced onto the Plains?

Horses arrive in America

In 1680, Pueblo Indians of the South West desert area revolted against the Spaniards who were in control of their land. Many people were killed and many horses were left ownerless. After this date, horses quickly spread northwards from tribe to tribe.

There were four ways that a tribe could increase its number of horses. An Indian could, for example, trade eagle feathers or buffalo robes for horses. Horses could also be captured and tamed from the wild. Sometimes they could be bred within the tribe. However, most tribes of the Plains liked to get horses by going on horse raids.`

Source A

'At daybreak, the Sioux watched the Shoshoni [a nearby tribe] turn their horses out to graze. As the last of the horses were leaving the water, the Sioux rode down and surrounded the herd and headed north–east to their camp. Over one hundred Shoshoni ponies had been captured.'

Arnold Iron Shell of the Sioux, from R. B. Hassrick, *The Sioux*, 1964

Lives changed by horses

Not all tribes took to horses. Some only used them occasionally or simply ate them. But the Sioux, along with other Plains tribes, built their whole lifestyle around horses. Look at the following information and think about the changes that came about because of the spread of horses.

Food

On horseback, the Sioux Indians were able to chase and catch many more buffalo than before. They could also travel further to good hunting grounds, which resulted in a better-fed tribe. But it also meant that the numbers of buffalo started to go down, with some tribes occasionally killing hundreds in one day. With so much meat, the Sioux tribes did not need to grow crops and they soon lost their farming skills.

Source B

'The Indian, mounted on his trained horse, dashes off at full speed among the herds of buffaloes, elks, or even antelopes, and deals his deadly arrows to their hearts from his horse's back. The horse is the fastest animal on the plains, and easily brings his rider alongside his victims.'

George Catlin, *Manners, Customs and Conditions of the North American Indians*, 1832–1839

Trade and travel

The horse-mounted Sioux could now travel much greater distances. As they travelled further, they were able to meet and trade with more people. New trade brought new items, such as metal bowls and knives, into their possession. Long-distance travel had its disadvantages as well. As the Sioux entered new lands, they often gained new enemies among the local tribes.

Homes

Before the horse, Indians had relied on dogs to help them carry their belongings, which limited the amount of goods they could own and the size of the tepee. Because horses could carry more, tepees grew from being 5–6 feet high to 12–15 feet. The luggage was attached to two long poles that were fixed to the horse's sides. This was known as a travois and could carry old or sick people who, in the past, might have been left behind to die when the camp moved on .

Women

Horses helped to improve the status of women in the tribe. As the horses took over much of the heavy work, particularly when moving camp, the women had more time to spend on highly valued hand crafts. Women could also own horses and many became skilled riders.

War

A fast and fearless horse was a warrior's most prized possession. Although the horse gave the Indian warrior new opportunities to show his bravery, it also meant that some tribes became more aggressive and fighting became more likely.

Source D

'My horse be swift in flight
Even like a bird;
My horse be swift in flight,
Bear me now in safety
Far from the enemy's arrows,
And you shall be rewarded
With streamers and ribbons red.'

Sioux warrior's song to his horse, nineteenth century

◄ Source C

A Plains Indian family moving camp.

This map shows ▼ how horses spread throughout the Plains.

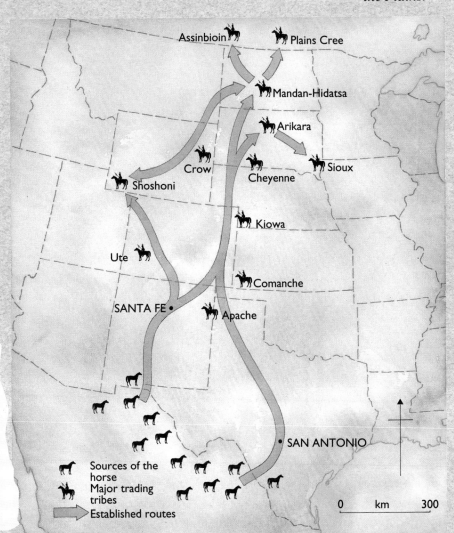

Sources of the horse
Major trading tribes
Established routes

0   km   300

1 What caused the horse to spread across the Plains?

2 In what ways did horses improve the lives of the Plains Indians?

3 What, if any, were the bad effects of horses on the Plains Indians?

4 Imagine an old Indian, who doesn't like the changes brought about by horses, arguing with a younger horse lover of the same tribe. In pairs, make up a script of the argument they have.

5 In what ways do you think that life after the horse might have been the same as life before the horse?

on

8

Life in an Indian camp

> The Sioux moved camp five or six times in a year. Wherever they settled, the women worked hard at making life comfortable, from making the tepees to producing intricate beadwork and quilling.
>
> What was life like in the camp, especially for women?

Inside a tepee

Much of the tepee floor was covered with buffalo robes, hair side up. Beds, also made from buffalo robes, were placed around the edge of the tepee. Storage bags were kept between the beds or hung on the poles along with a water bag and the weapons and costume of the warrior. There was little in the way of furniture. The smoke hole at the top could be moved according to the direction of the wind. In summer, the bottom edge of the tepee could be raised to make it cooler. In winter, a tepee lining kept the home warm.

The tepee was undoubtedly very well adapted for the nomadic life of the Sioux tribes. It was easy to take down and put up. Women could take down their homes within fifteen minutes. The long poles could be strapped to dogs and horses and the cover could be packed away into quite a small bundle.

- Why do you think that the Sioux owned so few things?

Source A

A white American describes the living conditions of tepees that he visited:

'The fire is built in the centre, and the smoke escapes through a hole at the top. The draught is, however, very poor, and in cold weather the tepee is usually too full of smoke to be bearable to anyone but an Indian. In this small space are often crowded eight or ten persons. Since the cooking, eating, living and sleeping are all done in the one room, it soon becomes unbelievably dirty.'

Colonel Richard Dodge, *Hunting Grounds of the Great West*, 1877

Colonel Dodge admitted that the tepee was well suited to the needs of the Indians but he found it an unpleasant place to live in. Many others, such as the Sioux chief, Flying Hawk, disagreed.

Source B

'The tepee is much better to live in; always clean, warm in winter, cool in summer; easy to move. Indians and animals know better how to live than white man; nobody can be in good health if he does not have all the time fresh air, sunshine and good water. If the Great Spirit wanted men to stay in one place he would make the world stand still; but He made it to always change.'

Flying Hawk, 1852–1931

Working women

Tepee-making was the job of women. It required not just hard work, but also a great deal of skill. The tepee was made of buffalo hides. After long hours of scraping, softening and stretching the hides, they had to be carefully cut and sewn together. The average tepee required about 18–20 hides and a woman needed the help of her female relatives.

Food

Women on the Plains collected a variety of wild roots, berries, seeds and plants to serve with their meat. Before the Indians traded for metal pots, they mixed stews in strong bags made out of buffalo stomach lining and added red-hot stones to make the stew boil. Boiled meat was also dried and ground with cherries and fat into a nutritious paste called pemmican. This could be stored in rawhide containers and kept for the winter months when food supplies were much lower. The diet of the Plains Indians was generally well balanced. They often ate three meals a day and starvation was only experienced in the harshest winters.

Source C

A nineteenth-century painting by George Catlin of women dressing a buffalo hide outside their tepees.

- *What things might the women make from the buffalo hide?*

1 Why do you think that the authors of Sources A and B disagree about tepee life?

2 How useful are these sources for telling us about life in a tepee?

3 Write down the good and bad things about living in a tepee, in two columns, under the headings Good and Bad.

Source D

Women on the Plains did many other jobs around the camp. An Indian woman from a neighbouring tribe to the Sioux describes her work below. A Sioux woman would probably have given a similar list of tasks:

'We women had our children to care for, meat to cook and to dry, robes to dress, skins to tan, clothes, tepees and moccasins to make. Besides these things we not only pitched the lodges, but took them down and packed the horses and the travois when we moved camp; yes, and we gathered the wood for our fires too.'

Pretty Shield, an Indian woman of the Crow tribe, late nineteenth century

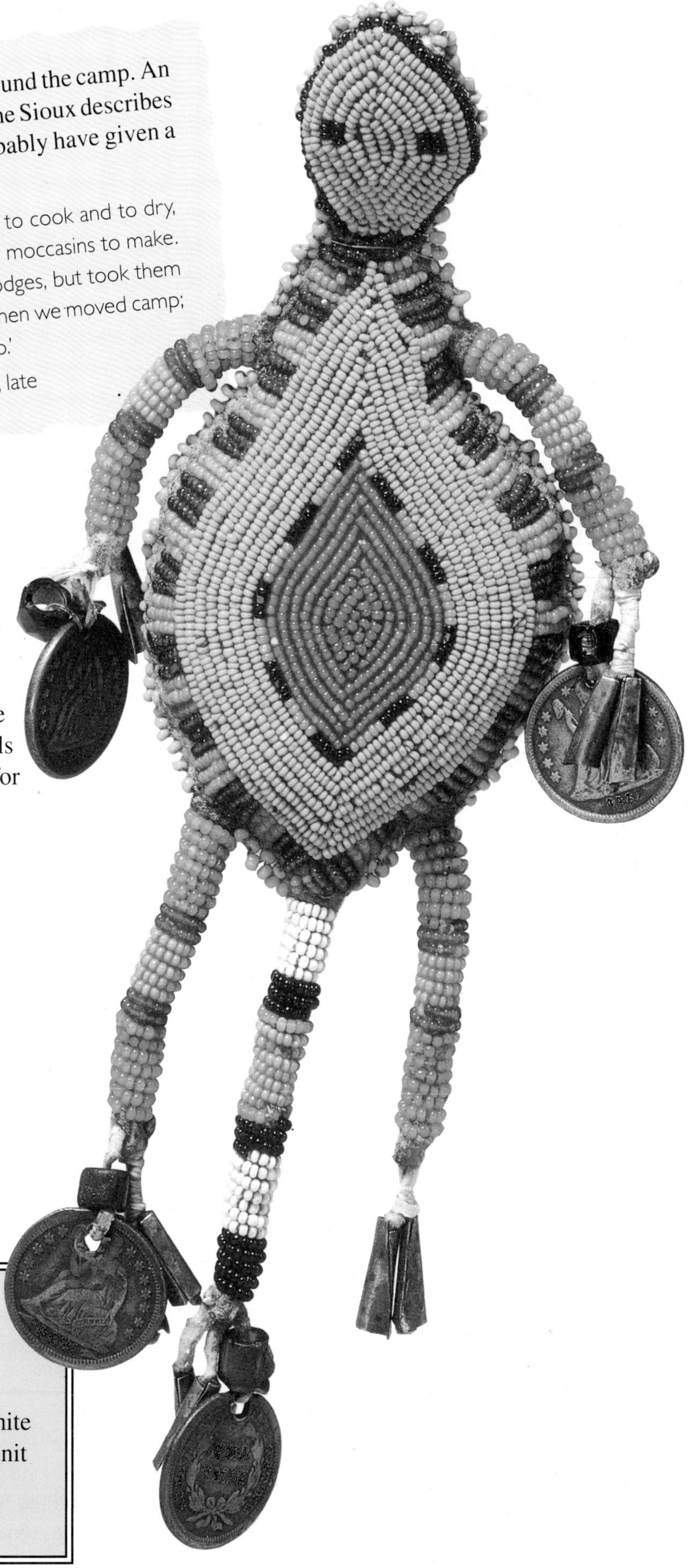

Crafts

Craft skills were very highly valued amongst the Sioux and a talented woman could achieve great status through her work. Beadwork and making clothes were important but quilling was the greatest skill of a craftswoman. Porcupine quills were dyed and woven into beautiful patterns for decorating clothes and other items.

Source E ▶

This amulet is a beaded bag containing the umbilical cord of a baby. Indians believed that such objects helped to ensure long life.

4 'Women were as important as men in the life of the camp.' Do you agree with this statement? Use evidence to back up your answer.

5 Indians were often described as savages by white people. What evidence could you use from this unit to argue against this description?

31

Living off the buffalo

The buffalo was not an easy animal to catch. It was large, strong and very fast. Men of the Plains tribes risked their lives trying to catch it because it could provide all the basic needs of life, as well as many luxuries.

How did the Sioux Indians use the buffalo?

George Catlin

The artist and explorer, George Catlin, spent over six years from 1832 to 1839 amongst the tribes of the Plains, travelling by horse and boat. In 1832, he visited the Sioux Indians and recorded their lives in words and paintings. In his book he tells us a lot about Sioux hunting and their uses of the buffalo.

Source A

A buffalo hunt painted by George Catlin, 1832.

Buffalo hunt

By surrounding a herd of buffalo, Indians could kill all of them in about 15 minutes. It was noisy and dangerous as the confused animals ran around in a circle of panic.

Source B

George Catlin joined in some Sioux hunts and watched many more. This is how he described them:

'When chasing a large herd, the Indian generally rides close in the rear, until he selects the animal he wishes to kill, which he separates from the crowd as soon as he can, by dashing his horse between it and the herd, and forcing it off by itself where he can approach it without the danger of being trampled to death. For the beginner, there is much danger to his limbs and life. For the Indian who has made this the everyday sport and amusement of his life, there is less difficulty and less danger.'

George Catlin, *Manners, Customs and Conditions of the North American Indians*, 1832–1839

• What are the main dangers of this kind of hunting?

Using the buffalo

Once the animals had been killed, the women came in to skin and butcher them where they lay. The women carried their meat and skins home, where they put them to a great variety of uses. The thick strong skin of old bulls was used for shields and winter moccasins. The thin skin of a calf was made into underclothes and tobacco pouches. Buffalo fat was used for soap, and the rough side of the tongue was used for hairbrushes.

Source C

George Catlin describes more of the uses of the buffalo.

'Every part of their flesh is converted into food. The skins are worn by the Indians and are used as coverings for their tepees and beds. The horns are shaped into spoons; their bones are used for war clubs and scrapers; their sinews are used for strings and backs to their bows and for thread to string their beads and sew their dresses. The feet of the animals are boiled, with their hooves, for glue. The hair from the head is twisted and braided into halters and the tail is used for a fly brush.'

George Catlin, *Manners, Customs and Conditions of the North American Indians*, 1832–1839

An uncertain future

In late summer, George Catlin saw such large herds of buffalo that the Plains looked black for miles but he was worried about their future. He saw that Indians were killing many more than they needed so that they could trade their skins for European goods such as knives, guns and other metal objects. He also knew that the white people in the East were moving closer to the Plains.

Source D

'The buffalo's doom is sealed, and with their extinction, the Indians must surely sink into despair and starvation. The Plains offer them no other means of living.'

George Catlin, *Manners, Customs and Conditions of the North American Indians*, 1832–1839

Source E

Buffalo bull dance of the Mandan tribe, painted by George Catlin.

---

1 Write your own eyewitness account of a buffalo hunt.

2 Do you think that George Catlin is a good source for finding out about the Sioux buffalo hunt? Give reasons for your answer.

3 Can you think of any reasons why his sources might not be accurate?

4 How important was the buffalo to the Sioux Indians? Use evidence from the sources to back up your answer.

Growing up the Sioux way

The birth of a child was celebrated with great joy in a Sioux camp. Each new life added to the strength of the band.

What was life like for Sioux children as they were growing up?

The birth of a baby

Although they married young — between the ages of about 12 and 15 — Sioux women gave birth, on average, to only three or four children. The birth usually took place in the woman's own tepee, with her mother and perhaps another woman of the tribe to help. The risks of child birth must have been high but the hard-working women were fit and coped well. Shortly after birth, the child was given a name by a respected older man or woman of the tribe. Usually they named the child after an animal or a brave deed or dream of their own. A boy might change his name when he was older, following a special dream or vision.

Family life

The Sioux Indians lived in large family groups that included all generations — young and old. A child would call its aunts and uncles 'mother' and 'father' as well as its parents.

Games and learning

Sioux children did not go to school; they learnt by copying adults in their games. Very small girls often played with deerskin dolls and toy tepees, while the boys often played with miniature bows and arrows. When they were a little older, the boys might hunt birds and rabbits and bring them back for the young girls to cook. At the age of six, a boy could ride and help with the horses and a girl could help dig vegetable roots and collect firewood. Both boys and girls had their own physical games. Sioux girls played a kind of hockey. Between the ages of 12 and 14, a boy would go on his first buffalo hunt. In these ways they learnt all that they needed to be an active member of the tribe.

Source A

A Sioux doll which shows a woman's costume and riding equipment in detail.

Getting married

Once boys and girls became teenagers, they were no longer allowed to play together. Before marriage, a young man and woman were not allowed to be alone together. The most privacy that they were allowed, when getting to know each other, was a blanket thrown around them outside the family tepee!

When a marriage took place the family of the bridegroom had to pay a bride-price to the bride's family. This might range from one horse to many horses, depending on the status of the bride's family. The marriage brought two families closer together. It gave their parents more certainty of being looked after in their old age by their children and grandchildren.

In most Indian societies, a man moved into the family of his new wife and his children became a part of that family. In Sioux society, the rules were not so strict and a newly married couple could move into either family.

Source B
Arnold Iron Shell, a Sioux chief, describes a proper Sioux marriage:

'There was this young man who wished to marry a girl. He asked her many times to run off with him, but she refused. Finally, he asked her if he might marry her. She told him to go home and tell his family to make a feast and that she would ask her parents.

So the young man went home and told his people, urging them that they must give a feast. His family agreed and took several fine horses over to her male relatives, and then they took clothes to the girl.

When the day of the feast came, the girl's male relatives put her on a horse and led her over to the tepee of her bridegroom's parents. Many people came to the feast, but there was no speech. He wanted the girl so they gave her to him.'

Arnold Iron Shell, Brule Sioux Chief

Source C
Young girls often had the job of looking after babies and very small children. This baby, like all Plains babies, is strapped into a cradleboard which could be hung up or leant against something, giving the baby a good view of the world around. These elaborate boards were usually made by a female relative of the father.

Sometimes a wealthy man might have more than one wife. Successful hunters brought home a lot of work and it was often desirable that this work should be shared amongst more than one wife. Many men were killed in war and hunting, leaving more women than men. Multiple marriages seemed to be a sensible solution.

If a marriage did not work well, divorce was easy for either partner. The man could do it by banging a drum and announcing it to the tribe and the woman could do it by simply moving all her belongings back to her parents' tepee.

---

1 Write down some differences between the way you have grown up and the way a Sioux child grew up.

2 What kind of education did Sioux children have?

3 In Source B, who takes responsibility for making the bride's arrangements?

4 Why did some men have more than one wife?

35

The spirit of life

The beliefs and ceremonies of the Sioux have been well recorded, both by the Sioux themselves and by their visitors.

What can we learn about Sioux religion from these sources?

The Great Spirit

To the Indians the world was full of mysteries. They did not use scientific ideas to explain the weather or the seasons or any other physical forces of nature. They noticed these changes and events and saw them as part of the mystery world of spirits and they paid particular attention to dreams, which they believed gave them knowledge and power.

Wakan tanka

The Sioux believed that the sun, the earth, the sky, the mountains, the animals and all the things around them possessed a spirit which they should worship. All of these spirits were controlled by the Great Spirit, known as 'Wakan tanka'. This literally meant 'great mystery'.

Source A

An old Teton Sioux explains the works of Wakan tanka:

'Plants are sent by Wakan tanka and come from the ground at his command. Wakan tanka teaches the birds to make nests. The stones and minerals are placed in the ground by Wakan tanka.'

Okute, speaking in 1911

Source B

The Indian world was carefully organised in sacred patterns, of which the circle was the most important.

'You have noticed that everything an Indian does is in a circle, and that this is because the Power of the World works in circles. The sun comes up and goes down again in a circle. The moon does the same, and both are round. Even the seasons form a great circle and always come back to where they were. The life of a man is a circle from childhood to childhood.'

Black Elk, of the Oglala Sioux, who was born in 1863

Religion

All Indians believed in spirits which could bring evil or good to the tribe. The Sioux spent much of their lives trying to please the spirits to get their help. Religious worship was a part of everyday life.

Source C – Prayer

'In the life of the Indian there is only one duty — the duty of prayer. His daily devotions are more necessary to him than daily food. He wakes at day break and steps down to the water's edge. After the bath, he stands before the advancing dawn, facing the sun. Each soul must meet the morning sun, the new sweet earth and the Great Silence alone.

Ohiyesa, of the Santee Sioux, 1911

Ceremonies

The Sioux performed many dances and rituals for the spirits. According to George Catlin, they seemed to have a dance for everything. The most sacred of their ceremonies was called 'Looking at the Sun'. This involved a great deal of pain for those taking part and was the highest form of worship for a Sioux. The ceremony was carried out to make sure that the power of the sun would come back each day. Anyone doing it was given great power and respect within the tribe, if he was able to bear the pain for a full day.

Source D

A painting of the Looking at the Sun ceremony.

Power from the spirits

An individual hoped to gain special power from the spirits. A teenage Sioux boy would try to gain the power of a spirit through going on what the Sioux called a 'vision quest'. He went up into a hill and did not eat for up to six days. His body became weak and his imagination became strong. In this state, he would dream, and if he saw an animal or bird in his dream, it was believed that creature would become his special guardian spirit for the rest of his life. His dreams sometimes told him of plants that he must collect together and put in a bag as a charm. This was known as his medicine bundle and only he was allowed to touch it.

- Why do you think that the Indians thought that dreams were so important?

Medicine men and women

The Sioux, and other Indians, believed that some people in the tribe were especially good at dealing with the spirits. Each tribe had a special medicine man, second only in importance to the chief. He was in charge of all the ceremonies and was believed to have strong magical powers. An older married woman could, more rarely, become a medicine woman if she showed magical abilities. Their jobs included such things as telling the future, advising the tribe, casting love spells and healing the sick.

Plant medicines

Although much of the medicine man or woman's healing involved magical power, they also had a good knowledge of plants which could cure sicknesses. For example, the powdered roots of the skunk cabbage were successfully used to relieve asthma. The curing properties of 170 Indian drugs have been officially recognised in the USA.

---

1 What did the Sioux worship?

2 The white settlers brought Christianity to America from the fifteenth century onwards. Do you think that the Indians would have found any similarities between the Christian God and their own Wakan tanka?

3 What was the importance of the circle to Sioux life?

4 'The healing of the medicine man was based only on superstition.' Do you agree with this statement?

5 Choose one source which you think gives the best idea of what Sioux religion was like. Explain your choice.

Plants with curing properties.

Talking and writing

Writing was not a part of the Indian tradition and before the Europeans came and gave Indians the idea of writing, Indian languages were spoken only. Despite this, Indians were able to communicate with each other in a number of ways.

How was information passed between Indians?

Storytelling

The Sioux, like other Indians, took great pleasure in an evening of storytelling and in this way tribal stories and traditions were passed down by word of mouth. Stories of brave deeds from the past and mysterious myths were always popular.

Source A

Charles Russell made this painting of an Indian storyteller in the 1880s. Old Indian men held their audiences spellbound for many hours. Notice the sacred pipe on the floor in front of the storyteller.

Writing in pictures

For the Sioux, the nearest thing to writing, before the middle of the nineteenth century, was their use of pictures and symbols to represent events such as those used on the buffalo robe calendar shown in Source C. Camp life and battles were sometimes recorded in this way.

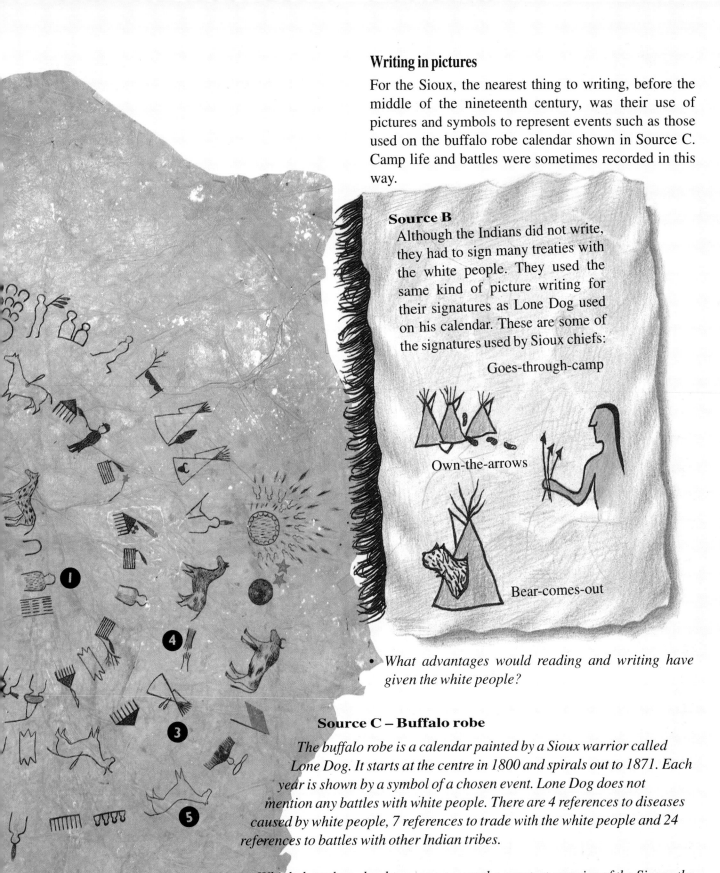

Source B

Although the Indians did not write, they had to sign many treaties with the white people. They used the same kind of picture writing for their signatures as Lone Dog used on his calendar. These are some of the signatures used by Sioux chiefs:

Goes-through-camp

Own-the-arrows

Bear-comes-out

• *What advantages would reading and writing have given the white people?*

Source C – Buffalo robe

The buffalo robe is a calendar painted by a Sioux warrior called Lone Dog. It starts at the centre in 1800 and spirals out to 1871. Each year is shown by a symbol of a chosen event. Lone Dog does not mention any battles with white people. There are 4 references to diseases caused by white people, 7 references to trade with the white people and 24 references to battles with other Indian tribes.

• *Which does the calendar suggest were the greatest enemies of the Sioux: the white people or other Indian tribes?*

• *In small groups try to explain the meaning of the five numbered symbols on the buffalo robe. Copy each symbol into your book and write what you think it might mean beside your drawing. Leave a small amount of space after each explanation.*

39

Sign language

Tribes on the Plains were able to understand each other, no matter what their language, by speaking with their hands and arms. The language was made up of many words and was understood over a very wide area. They also passed messages over long distances by the use of smoke signals.

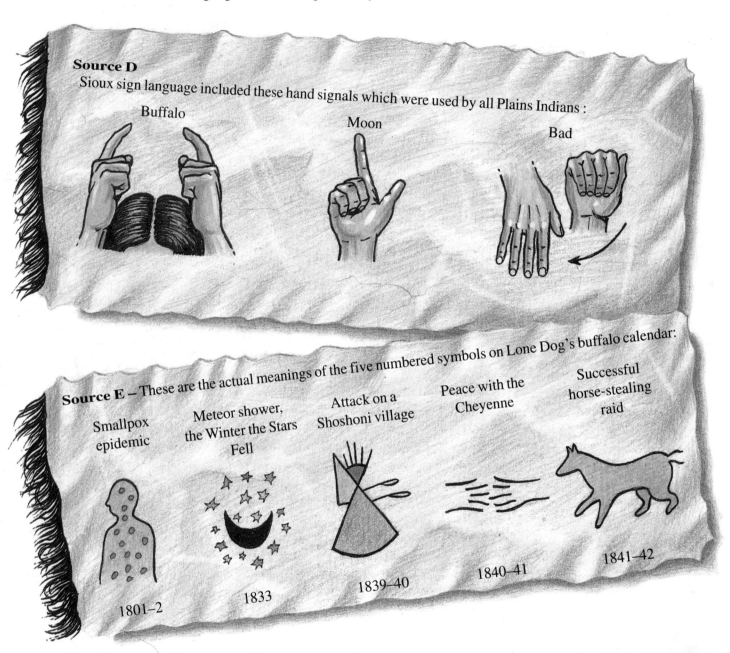

Source D

Sioux sign language included these hand signals which were used by all Plains Indians:

Buffalo

Moon

Bad

Source E — These are the actual meanings of the five numbered symbols on Lone Dog's buffalo calendar:

Smallpox epidemic

Meteor shower, the Winter the Stars Fell

Attack on a Shoshoni village

Peace with the Cheyenne

Successful horse-stealing raid

1801–2

1833

1839–40

1840–41

1841–42

---

1 Write an account of what you did on your last birthday using only pictures and symbols — no words! Swap stories with a neighbour and try to write a description of their day. How accurate were your descriptions? Were there any misunderstandings?

2 Look at Source E and compare the explanation given there to your own ideas of what the symbols might mean. Against your explanation write the real meaning of the symbol. How close did you get to the real meaning?

3 You probably found it difficult to guess what the symbols meant. Do you think that historians should guess about events from one source like this? Explain your answer.

13

Warriors and weapons

The Plains were vast open spaces where tribes only rarely saw their neighbours. Yet warfare between them was common. Some tribes, including the Sioux, would actually look for opportunities to fight.

Why was war so important on the Plains?

Warrior societies

Bravery in war was the best way for a man to win honour. He therefore welcomed the opportunities that war brought. Most boys longed for the day when they could become members of a warrior society. Each society had its own costumes, songs and dances, and organised war raids against their enemies. Each society expected loyalty and great bravery from its members.

Source A
Song of the Sioux's Fox Warrior Society:

'I am a Fox
I am supposed to die.
If there is anything difficult,
If there is anything dangerous,
That is mine to do.'

Counting coups

The greatest sign of bravery during battle was to touch an enemy with either bare hands or a special long stick called a coup stick. The warrior societies ran a sort of point-scoring system for these blows or 'coups', as they came to be called. Acts of bravery were often more important than killing the enemy. A warrior would gain few points for killing a man from a distance with his bow and arrow but would gain maximum points for getting close enough to tap him with his coup stick.

Having counted his coups, the Indian would proudly display them for all to see. The usual way of recording coups was by the addition of feathers to their war bonnets or by notches on their coup sticks.

Source B

Plains warrior dressed for war and carrying a feathered coup stick. It is easy to see how this colourful costume could become the stereotype for all Indians.

The causes of war

Indians of the Plains were often keen to find a reason to fight so that they might win glory. Sometimes a war started as a result of an individual seeking revenge. Arnold Iron Shell describes one such case below.

Source C
'Shot-in-the-Heel's son, Holy Circle, had been killed in war against the Shoshoni tribe. Iron Shell, his brother, decided to take revenge for his death. He invited Holy Circle's warrior society to join him and a war party was organised.'
Arnold Iron Shell

41

Fighting for horses

The most common cause of war was Indians wanting horses or goods belonging to another tribe. Capturing horses from an enemy camp was a highly valued act of bravery. Occasionally tribes fought each other over the control of hunting grounds but this was unusual because the Indians did not see the land as their property. They never fought with the idea of conquering another tribe.

Other causes of war might include a real or imagined insult from another tribe or it might simply occur as a result of a dream.

Preparation for war

Having decided on war, the warriors spent time preparing themselves and their horses. It was a time of religious ritual and spiritual advice from the medicine man.

Source D
Arnold Iron Shell described the equipment needed for war:

'In saddle bags they put their leggings, their bone breast plates and their bladder food bags containing pemmican. Feathered war bonnets were also packed. They also brought new make-up kits packed with elk grease and paint, a porcupine tail brush, their pipes and pipe bags and a buffalo horn drinking cup.'

Arnold Iron Shell

Method of war

Sudden surprise raids were the Indians' favourite form of battle. These gave them plenty of opportunity for bravery and cunning but lessened their chances of being killed. An average of 10–30 Indians went on these raids and few were killed. Women very rarely took part in a raid although a few instances have been recorded. They were, however, quick to take up arms if their own camp was under attack.

Scalping

Death on the battlefield sometimes led to scalping. Without a scalp (skin and hair from the top of his head), the Sioux believed that a person could not enter the eternal after-life, known as 'the land of the many tepees'. Indians removed the scalp of their dead enemies so that they would have fewer enemies in the after-life. Europeans were horrified by the practice of scalping. Many felt that this showed the Indian to be truly savage. For the Sioux, a scalp was a prized trophy and a cause for great celebration.

Source E

Part of a war record of a Sioux warrior, Monka-ush-ka, painted on buffalo skin in about 1830. The picture shows the Sioux fighting Crow Indians, who can be identified by their long hairstyles.

- *What does the picture tell us about warfare on the Plains?* ▼

Weapons old and new

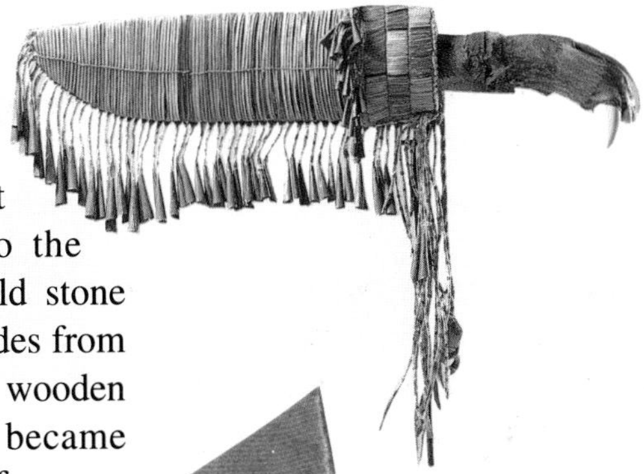

Before the middle of the nineteenth century, Plains Indians made their weapons from stone, bone and wood but as white traders came onto the Plains, metal replaced the old stone heads. Indians bought the blades from traders and made their own wooden handles. Steel knives also became available and were used for scalping and stabbing, as well as for more domestic purposes.

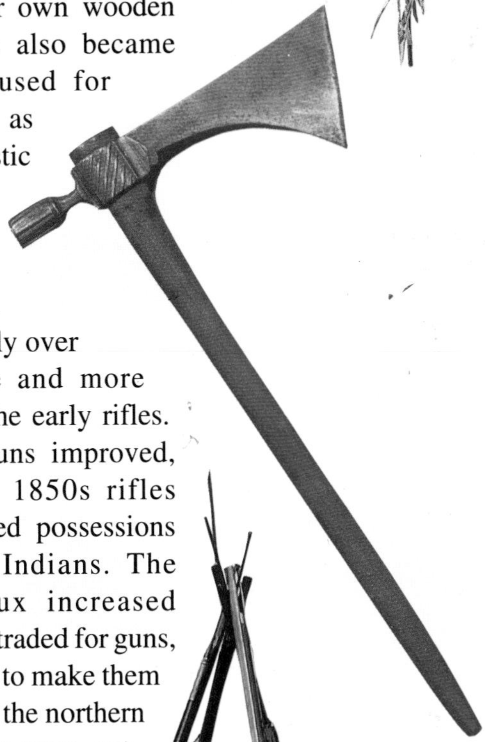

The bow and arrow was a very efficient weapon. It could be fired accurately over a long distance and more rapidly than the early rifles. However, guns improved, and by the 1850s rifles became prized possessions amongst the Indians. The power of the Sioux increased enormously when they traded for guns, their firepower helping to make them the dominant people of the northern Plains. But the Indians were not able to mend their rifles when they broke, nor could they make their own gunpowder or bullets. The gun made Indians more dependent on the white people and their technology so the traditional weapons continued to be used alongside the new.

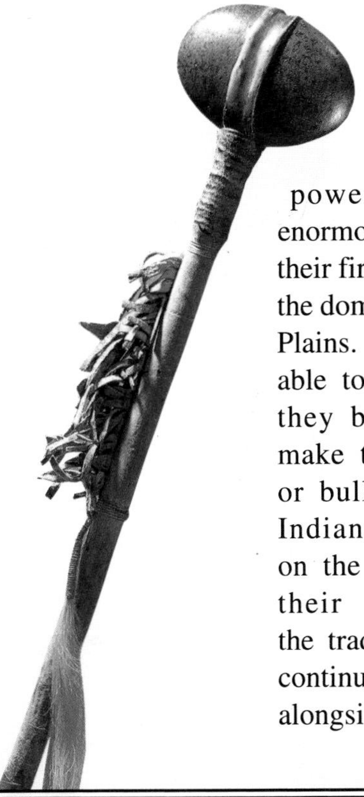

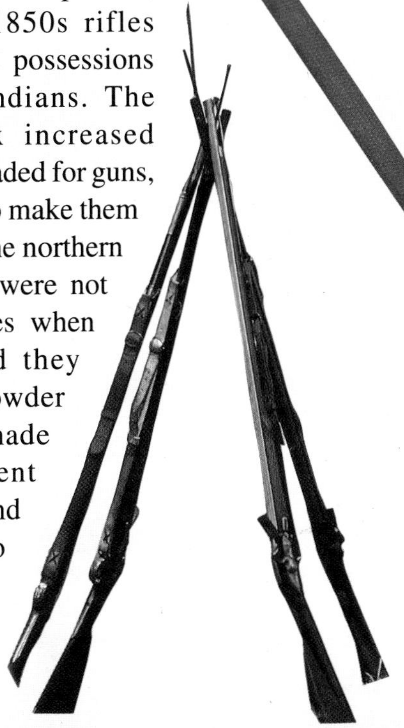

---

1 Why do you think that boys were so keen to join a warrior society?

2 For what reasons did the Plains Indians go to war?

3 Battles were quite frequent on the Plains. What effect do you think that they would have had on the population of the Indian tribes?

4 In what ways did Indian weapons change and in what ways did they stay the same?

5 Do you think that the Indians were better off with their new weapons?

43

North America—

The Sioux Indians and the white settlers were unable to live alongside each other. Their ways of life were very different, as were their feelings for the land and their hopes for the future. The Sioux would not surrender as some other tribes had done. They were strong in numbers and weapons and they decided that they must fight for what they believed was theirs.

The Indians and the United States in 1865

The map shows the extent to which the white people had taken over North America by 1865. Only the barren Plains and treacherous Rocky Mountains remained unconquered by the white Americans. Earlier in the century, the Indians of the east had been removed further and further away from the white towns, to be finally settled on the edge of the Plains in the Indian Territory — the present-day state of Oklahoma.

Although the Plains remained unconquered, the presence of the white people was felt strongly by 1865 as they sent their endless lines of wagons carrying settlers to the western coast. US army forts had been built to protect travellers and miners, and railways were being proposed. The balance of life on the Plains had been disturbed.

• Which wagon trails and railways passed through Sioux territory? Would the Indians have seen these changes as improvements?

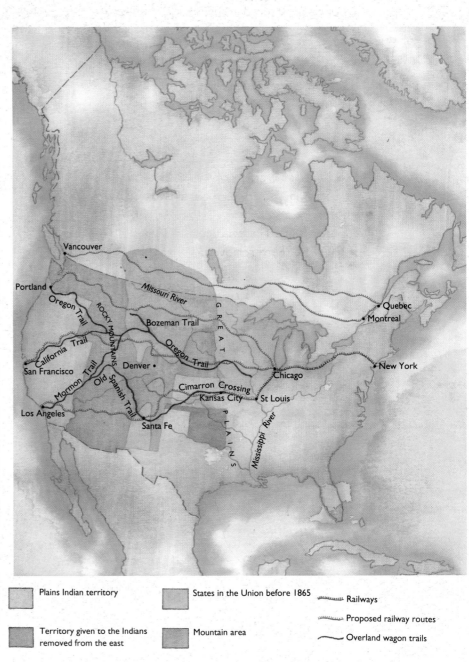

Plains Indian territory

Territory given to the Indians removed from the east

States in the Union before 1865

Mountain area

Railways

Proposed railway routes

Overland wagon trails

the struggle for land

1850–1860

Plains tribes let the United States government build roads and military posts on their land. In return, the Indians were promised that their land was theirs, forever. The Oregon wagon trail passes through Sioux lands.

1860–1864

Gold is discovered in the Rocky Mountains and a new trail called the Bozeman trail, is opened. It passes through the heart of Sioux hunting grounds. In 1862 two railroad companies receive permission to build railway lines across the Plains.

1864–1868

Red Cloud, a chief of the Oglala Sioux, leads a campaign of terror against travellers on the Bozeman trail and then defeats US soldiers. The Bozeman trail is closed and the military forts removed.

1868–1876

Many Sioux are not happy with the peace treaty and war starts again. In 1876 Sioux warriors defeat a detatchment of the US army at the Battle of the Little Bighorn.

1876–1890

The United States is outraged at the defeat and the government send in many more soldiers, who finally crush the Sioux rebels.

'The Death Struggle of General Custer' *by William Cary was used as a full-page picture in the* New York Daily Graphic, *19 July 1876. This newspaper had a wide readership in white America and the artist wanted to appeal to these people.*

Evidence

Evidence for the wars on the Plains is plentiful and varied. The world took an interest in the Sioux wars and many of the people directly involved had their say. The speeches of chiefs and army generals were recorded and newspapers told their stories, backed up with paintings and photographs. But in a situation of war, the artist's or author's support for one side may lead to less than the whole truth being told. Bias is common in the accounts of the Plains wars and the historian always needs to look out for it.

This beaded waistcoat, probably Sioux, shows an Indian view of fighting between a white man with a gun and an Indian.

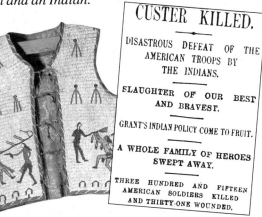

CUSTER KILLED.

DISASTROUS DEFEAT OF THE AMERICAN TROOPS BY THE INDIANS.

SLAUGHTER OF OUR BEST AND BRAVEST.

GRANT'S INDIAN POLICY COME TO FRUIT.

A WHOLE FAMILY OF HEROES SWEPT AWAY.

THREE HUNDRED AND FIFTEEN AMERICAN SOLDIERS KILLED AND THIRTY-ONE WOUNDED.

Newspaper headlines reporting the Battle of the Little Bighorn, New York World, *6 July, 1876.*

14

Upsetting the balance

The early European settlers had helped to create the Plains lifestyle by introducing horses. The descendants of these early white settlers brought guns and luxuries that were highly valued by the Indians. However, the gifts of the white people were not all good: with them also came many problems.

What problems did the new settlers bring to the Plains Indians?

Unhealthy trade

In the nineteenth-century Sioux diary of Arnold Iron Shell, each year is named after one important event. He called the years 1818, 1845 and 1850, 'smallpox'. Like many other deadly diseases, smallpox was brought to America from Europe. The Indians had no resistance to European diseases, and throughout the nineteenth century many thousands died of smallpox, cholera, and other European sicknesses. The Sioux suffered, although not as badly as some. The worst-hit tribe on the Plains was the Mandans, where only 31 people, out of a tribe of 1,600, survived the smallpox epidemic of 1837.

Wagons and trains

The first signs of a permanent change for the Sioux were the wagon trails that crossed their land. From the 1850s, many white settlers made the dangerous journey across the Plains in their covered wagons. They travelled to new homes in Oregon and California along a route called the Oregon trail. This passed through the southern part of the Sioux territory.

In the 1860s there were even more threatening changes as railroad, or railway, lines started to appear. The Indians realised that soon the great iron machines could bring thousands of new people on to the Plains.

Source A

Wagons on the Oregon trail.

Killing the buffalo

The Indians may have tolerated the passing wagons and steam trains if they had not been damaging their supply of buffalo. The trains not only frightened the animals away but they also brought new hunters onto the Plains whose powerful weapons were rapidly destroying the herds. The US government saw that without buffalo the Indians could not survive. They therefore encouraged white hunters to kill the herds so that the Indians would become weak and would have to surrender their rights to the land. Between 1840 and 1885, the buffalo became virtually extinct as its numbers fell from 13 million to 200 animals.

Source B

This engraving shows passengers shooting buffalo from their train. While professional hunters roamed the Plains for buffalo, passengers on the new railroads shot the animals for sport. Even the driver is taking a shot.

Source C

A US army general was asked whether something should be done to stop the buffalo hunters. He replied:

'For the sake of a lasting peace, let them kill, skin and sell until the buffaloes are exterminated.'

General Sheridan, 1872

Selling earth mother

Land was sacred to the Indians. They called it their 'earth mother'. She was the giver of life who could not be bought and sold. The Indians were horrified to see their earth mother being divided up and damaged by the ploughing, mining and building of the white people.

Source D

One Sioux chief said this about the white people:

'Hear me, people, we have now to deal with another race. Strangely enough they have a mind to plough the soil and the love of ownership is a disease with them. They claim this mother of ours, the earth, for their own; they deface her with their buildings and their refuse.'

Chief Sitting Bull of the Hunkpapa Sioux, 1877

Using the land

The growing population of the United States needed more land. By 1880 thousands of families had poured onto the Plains. The white settlers felt that the Indians were wasting the land by not cultivating it and that, because all the land was not being used all the time, they had a right to use it themselves. The Sioux, however, would not give up their land without fighting for it.

Source E

A white journalist gives his strong opinion of Indian land:

'As I passed over the very best cornlands on earth and saw their owners sitting around the doors of their lodges at the height of the planting season, I could not help saying, "These people must die out. God has given this earth to those who will tame and cultivate it."'

Horace Greeley, *An Overland Journey from New York to San Francisco*, 1859

---

1 What changes resulted from the arrival of white people on the Plains?

2 Which change do you think would have been the most damaging to the Indians?

3 What do you think was the result of these changes?

4 Why did the US government and army let the white hunters destroy the buffalo herds?

5 How do Sources D and E show the different feelings that white settlers and Indians had for the land?

6 The Indian chiefs were very good at making speeches. Imagine that you are a Plains Indian in the 1870s. Write a short speech to say how you feel about the recent changes in your lifestyle.

15

Sioux on the war path

The Sioux were one of the proudest and strongest of the Indian nations. They could not accept the demands of the white people who were moving onto their land in ever-increasing numbers.

How did the Sioux go to war?

Source A

Santee Indians on the day that the fighting started. This photograph, taken in 1862, shows the strange mixture of white and Indian culture on the Santee reservation.

• *How are the Indians trying to hold on to their own culture?*

Losing the land

Sioux tribes, such as the Santees on the eastern edge of the Plains, came into contact with white settlers much earlier than the Western Teton Sioux tribes. By 1851 the Santees had given up 24 million acres of hunting grounds. In return, the US government promised them annual payments and built them brick houses.

Trouble on the eastern Plains

Cheated out of money by unfair trading and close to starvation, a band of the Santee Sioux took to the war path when their annual payment from the government failed to arrive on time. In August 1862 about 400 warriors left their homes and set out on a rampage, killing about 450 white people in the neighbouring villages over a period of about four weeks.

Source B - The Minnesota massacre

This is one of a set of pictures of the Indian raid, painted by local artist John Stevens. It shows an Indian woman slashing the legs of a white girl in the presence of the child's mother. The pictures were published across the United States.

- *Do you think that the artist witnessed the scene in this picture? What effect would this picture have on the people who saw it?*

The white revenge

The US army were quickly called in, eventually defeating the rebellious Indians and their leader, Little Crow. Many of the white victims had been innocent of any crime and other white people were outraged at the Indians' actions. In response to public demand for revenge, 40 warriors were publicly hanged, more were imprisoned and many others, who had played no part in the fighting, were moved out to reservations further west. This fighting signalled the start of many Indian wars on the Plains.

Source C

War bonnet collected from Arapaho Chief Yellow Calf.

49

In the same year, further west, gold was discovered in the Rocky Mountains. A miner called John Bozeman opened up a trail for gold diggers which ran through the hunting grounds of the Western Sioux.

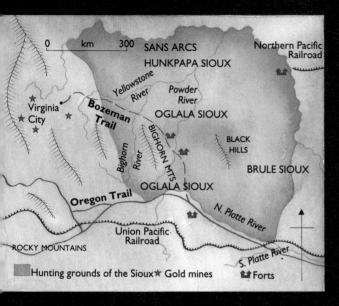

The Bozeman trail passing through Sioux hunting grounds.

Why would the Bozeman trail have worried the Sioux more than the Oregon trail?

Source D

Red Cloud addresses US government representatives at a council meeting:

'The Great Father [the US President] sends us presents and wants us to sell him the road, but the White Chief comes with soldiers to steal it before the Indian says yes or no. I will talk with you no more. I will go now and I will fight you!'

Red Cloud, 1866

Victory for the Teton Sioux

The Sioux, fearing a white invasion and the destruction of their buffalo herds, began attacking travellers on the Bozeman trail. In 1866 Red Cloud received news that the US government was planning to build forts along the trail. Many branches of the Teton Sioux joined together to fight the US army and after a fierce campaign the government tried to make peace with Red Cloud. The only peace term that he would accept was the closure of the Bozeman trail and so in June 1868 the troops were withdrawn and the Bozeman trail was closed. Red Cloud had won a great Indian victory. The peace treaty that he signed gave the Sioux a very large reservation area including all their hunting grounds, where no white people would be allowed to settle.

1 What were the consequences of white contact for the Santee Sioux?

2 What were the causes of Red Cloud's war? Try and divide them into long- and short-term causes.

3 What were the short-term consequences of Red Cloud's war for the Sioux Indians?

4 Write a short newspaper report on the Santee war or Red Cloud's war. Make it biased in favour of the Indians or the white settlers. Exchange your work with partners and work out who their reports favour.

Battle at Little Bighorn

In 1868, Red Cloud agreed to end his war and settle within a large reservation area but the peace did not last long. By 1876 the Sioux Indians and the US cavalry were fighting again.

Why did the Sioux Indians return to the war path?

Gold!

By 1872 more gold had been discovered in Sioux territory. This time the gold was in the Black Hills, a very sacred place to the Sioux and other Indians. Miners moved into the area and once again the peace of the Sioux was disturbed.

Source A

General Custer of the 7th Cavalry.

Source B

Black Elk of the Oglala Sioux explained how the fighting started again:

'It was when I was 11, in 1874, that the first sign of new trouble came to us. Scouts told us that many soldiers had come to the Black Hills. Afterwards I learnt that it was Long Hair [Custer]. He had no right to go there. The white men had made a treaty with Red Cloud that said it would be ours as long as the grass grows and water flows. Later I learned too that Long Hair had found much of the yellow metal that makes the white men crazy, and that is what made the bad trouble just as it did before.'

Black Elk, *Black Elk Speaks*

- Why do the Indians feel that the white men had no right to be in their territory?

51

Bloodshed at Little Bighorn

The US government asked the Sioux for permission to mine the gold, but they refused. The government was unable to stop miners going into the Black Hills and so the Indians dealt with them in their own way and many miners were killed. Soldiers were brought in to try to control the situation but the problems continued and, by 1876, the Sioux and the US army were prepared to fight.

Source C

Chief Sitting Bull of the Hunkpapa Sioux.

The Sioux were led by Chief Sitting Bull and Chief Crazy Horse, who were ready to fight the treaty breakers and refused to make any deals with the white people. In their camp in June 1876 there were not only Sioux Indians but also Cheyennes and Arapahos. Approximately 12,000 Indians had gathered at the Little Bighorn River. They were well armed and prepared for battle. When, on 25 June, the ambitious General Custer led his detachment of about 250 men of the 7th Cavalry towards the camp, he could not have realised the strength of the Indian force. The Indians struck down Custer and all his men that day.

Was it really a victory?

Victory at the Little Bighorn made Sitting Bull and Crazy Horse the most famous Indian chiefs. It was this victory, however, that finally broke the Sioux people. The US government was so shocked that they put huge amounts of money into a final effort to defeat the Indians. The fighting tribes were hunted down; some were killed, some surrendered and others escaped north to Canada.

Dancing for freedom

By the 1880s the Sioux were forced to live on reservations. Lacking the power to fight, they turned to their religion. They, and other Indians across America, started to perform a dance called the Ghost Dance. They believed that its magical powers would remove the white people and bring back the buffalo.

Source D

'Hear us and help us.

Take away the white men

Send back the buffalo

We are poor and weak

We can do nothing alone

Help us to be what we once

were —

Happy hunters of buffalo.'

Ghost Dance song, 1880s

The end for the Indians?

Although it was a peaceful dance, some Indians performed it holding rifles. This worried the government and the army. They were afraid that it would start up trouble again. In 1890 a group of largely unarmed Sioux ghost dancers were fired on by the 7th Cavalry. About 200 Indian men, women and children were killed. This became known as the Battle of Wounded Knee. It signalled the end of the Indians' hope for a return to the old life.

A modern artist's impression of the Ghost Dance.

Source E

This photograph, taken in 1890, shows Big Foot lying dead in the snow on the Wounded Knee battlefield. His frozen body represents the end of the Indian resistance.

1 What were the causes of the Battle of the Little Bighorn?

2 What were the short- and long-term consequences of the Battle of the Little Bighorn for the Sioux?

3 Why did the Indians perform the Ghost Dance in the 1880s?

4 What words would you use to describe the Indians' feelings as shown in Source D?

5 Why do you think that many Indians would have given up hope of returning to their old life after the Battle of Wounded Knee?

6 The US newspapers described the Little Bighorn as a massacre and Wounded Knee as a battle. Do you think that the Indians would have agreed with these words?

North America—

From the middle of the nineteenth century, areas of public land of varying sizes were put aside for the use of Indian tribes; each area is called a 'reservation'. Within the reservation, Indians were able to make some decisions about tribal life but overall control lay with the US government agents. The system of reservations was the United States' solution to the problem of what to do with the Indians as white people made their homes across America, but the Indians did not like their solution.

Indian reservations in the United States of America by the end of the nineteenth century

There were about 1 million Indians in North America at the time of their first contact with the Europeans. By the end of the nineteenth century there were only 250,000. These Indians, whose ancestors had once covered the whole of North America, were restricted to living in reservations, of which there were about 200. The same thing had happened in Canada, although it had been achieved with much less bloodshed. The Indian reserves, as they are known in Canada, are too many and too small to be shown on the map. Only in the frozen north did the native people avoid reservation life. The land was too cold for European settlements and so, although their lives were changed through contact with the whites, the Inuit were not removed to small reserves.

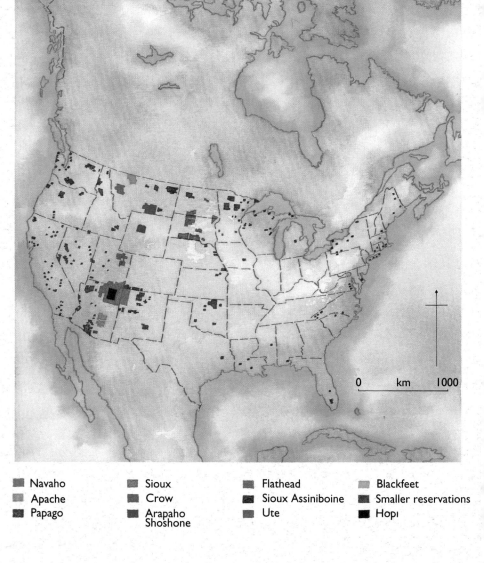

- Which tribes seem to have the largest reservations? Could the government have tried to settle the Indians in any other way?

0   km   1000

■ Navaho
■ Apache
■ Papago
■ Sioux
■ Crow
■ Arapaho Shoshone
■ Flathead
■ Sioux Assiniboine
■ Ute
■ Blackfeet
■ Smaller reservations
■ Hopi

land of the white people

1890–1920

The US government encourages the Indians to adopt white ways, such as schooling and farming. Indians do not like these changes and many ignore the government laws. The reservations get smaller as land within them is divided up and some is sold to white settlers.

1920–1960

The government gives citizenship to all Indians and allows them to renew tribal traditions. They are given more power to govern themselves on the reservations.

1960s and 1970s

Indians draw attention to the broken treaties of the past and their present problems through public protests.

1970s and 1980s

Some tribes were awarded large sums of money by the US law courts as compensation for their lost lands. The Sioux received $ 122.5 million for the loss of the Black Hills in 1877. Many would prefer to have the land returned rather than the money.

Present day

Some reservations make good money from activities such as mining and tourism but on the whole the Indians are much poorer, in money and health, than other people in the USA and the Indian population is increasing quite rapidly. Many have moved to the cities to look for work.

Evidence

Twentieth-century history provides a vast range of sources. More records have been kept and improved technology means that information can get passed on more easily. More Indian sources are available because their languages have become written languages. Many Indians have felt it important that they should speak up about their experiences. This helps to balance our evidence with the views of the white Americans.

This is the death mask of Ishi, the lone survivor of a group of prehistoric Indians, who had had no contact with white people until he was found starving in 1911. Anthropologists learned a great deal from him about tool-making – some of those he made are shown below – trap-setting, plants and all the rituals and taboos of an Indian hunter's life.

Today many traditions are preserved by Indian tribes who continue to celebrate their ancient rituals and customs such as this potlach ceremony. During a potlach members of the tribe bring honour on themselves and demonstrate their generosity by giving away many of their possessions.

Hopi Navajo Indians protesting against government take-over of their land.

Adapting to reservation life

When all the wars were over, the Indians had no choice but to accept reservation life. By 1890 all Indians were settled on reservations. There were many new problems for them to face.

How well did the Indians adapt to their new lifestyle?

Source A

This painting by W.R.Leigh shows an Indian ploughing the land and gazing at a buffalo skull.

- *What impression is the artist trying to create by showing the Indian looking at the buffalo skull?*

The reservation land

Look at the map of reservations on the previous page. Compare it with the map on page 8. What kinds of land are most of the reservations on?

The Mescalero Apache Indians of the South West Plains were moved on eight times before they were finally allowed to settle in one place. Fertile land or the discovery of valuable minerals attracted white settlers into the Indian territories. By the end of the nineteenth century, the reservations were not only smaller but they were also on the most infertile land. The land that nobody else wanted was left to the Indians.

Farming the land

On these barren lands, the Indians were now expected to make a living by farming. US government officials gave advice on farming methods and gave the Indians farming tools, and sometimes cattle.

Lost traditions

For the Indians of the Plains, farming had been only a very small part of their tradition. In some of the hunting tribes, a little farming had been carried out by the women. The glory that men had gained through hunting and fighting was gone and farming was a poor replacement. They had no wish to become farmers and felt great despair at their loss.

Source B

Ration day on a reservation in the late nineteenth century. Indians had to queue for their ration of foods and other goods, given to them by the US government. Sometimes the rations were late or did not arrive. Starvation was, therefore, not uncommon.

Failure

In many reservations the soil was poor and many Indians were put off farming by early crop failures. Many saw these failures as a sign from nature or the Great Spirit that they were not meant to farm. Ploughing up the land in this way went against their beliefs in the sacredness of mother earth.

Poor soils and a lack of farming knowledge meant that very few Indians could provide enough food for their families. Without the buffalo, they were unable to make their own clothes and tools. For all these things, they depended on rations from the government. The tribes could no longer look after themselves, but depended on gifts from their former enemies.

Source D

George Bird Grinnell describes how Pawnee Indians adapted to life on the reservation in Oklahoma:

'During the first four years of their stay in Oklahoma the condition of the Pawnees was most miserable. The wretched condition continued up to about 1885. By then they came to realise that it was absolutely necessary for them to go to work if the tribe was to continue to exist. They began to work; at first only a few, but gradually many. A point was reached when it was no longer necessary to issue them government rations. They raised enough on their farms to support themselves. Nowadays by far the greater number of Pawnees wear civilised clothing, ride in wagons and send their children to the agency school.'

Scribner, *Pawnee Hero Stories and Folk Tales,* 1890

Source C

Santanta, chief of the Kiowa Indians, describes how he feels about moving to a reservation:

'I have heard that you intend to settle us on a reservation near the mountains. I don't want to settle. I love to roam over the prairies. There I feel free and happy, but when we settle down we grow pale and die.'

Santanta, Kiowa chief, 1860s

Declining population

For most tribes the change to reservation life was not as successful as Grinnell described. Many Indians died of illnesses and starvation. The American Indian population fell quite dramatically in the last two decades of the nineteenth century. Some small tribes disappeared altogether. As the twentieth century approached, the future of the Indians looked doubtful.

Walking the white road

Once all Indians were on reservations, the United States government tried to make them live like white people.

The drawing of the Pine Ridge Reservation gives an idea of how quickly the Indian lifestyle changed. Twenty years earlier, the Sioux chief, Red Cloud, had been fighting the US army over Sioux land rights. Now he lived in a government-built home, flying the United States flag. The different types of building give us an idea of the kinds of thing that the government provided for the Indians.

Providing for the Indians

The United States government were afraid that if they allowed the Indians to run their own lives they would either die because they could not farm successfully or they would rebel against government authority. It was the second of these fears which made the government bring in laws to try to force the Indians to live like white people.

How to make a white man

Between 1880 and 1920 the American government attempted to change the Indian way of life in the following ways:

- Indian children were sent to boarding or day schools where they would learn the ways of the white people by wearing their clothes and learning their subjects and their language.

- In 1887 the government introduced a law that gave each Indian family 160 acres of land. They wanted to encourage the Indians to become independent farmers like the white families, which would break down their loyalty to the tribe. But the Indians did not want to be farmers and many sold off their acres to white people. Once again Indian lands were shrinking.

- In the early twentieth century, government officials said that Indian men must cut their hair and that men and women should not paint their faces. Those who broke these rules could not get jobs on the reservation. Tribal dances and ceremonies were also made illegal.

- The Church also played a part in trying to change the Indians', religion. Many did adopt Christianity, usually in addition to their traditional beliefs and ceremonies.

American citizens

It was not until 1924 that the US government began to recognise the rights of Indians as individual people. In that year all Indians were given citizenship of the United States. This meant that they could vote and be fully protected by US law. This was largely because of the part played by many Indians who had fought in the American army during the First World War (1914–18).

In 1934 the government gave up their policy of selling off strips of reservation land and they stopped trying to encourage Indians to give up their traditional culture. The United States at last showed real signs of accepting Indian culture as part of their heritage.

Source E
The picture on page 59 shows a modern artist's impression of the Pine Ridge Sioux Reservation Agency in 1885. You can identify the numbered buildings from the list below:

1 boarding school,
2 council room and doctor's office,
3 storehouse,
4 police quarters,
5 employees' quarters,
6 agent's quarters,
7 interpreter's quarters,
8 stable and ration issue centre,
9 ice and meat house,
10 water works,
11 oil house,
12 Chief Red Cloud's house.

- What kind of services did the government provide on the reservations?

1 Using an atlas and the map on page 54, write down the names of five states which have a lot of reservation land and five states which have no reservations. Why do you think that there are almost no reservations east of the Mississippi River?

2 Why were many Indians not very successful at farming?

3 Draw a picture flow diagram to show how the government and others tried to change an Indian into a white person.

4 a How successful do you think that the attempted changes were?

b Would you agree that the lives of the Indians changed for the better between 1880 and 1920? Explain your answer.

5 Write a short play based on the scene in Source B. Include the following:

a a discussion between the government officials and the Indians receiving their rations

b a discussion between two or more of the Indians in the background that gives an idea of how they feel about their new life.

Indians today

During the twentieth century the numbers of Indians have increased. Many still live on reservations where they are free to keep up their tribal traditions. Others have moved away and adopted the white American lifestyle.

What is it like being an Indian in America today?

Tribal power

The Sioux of South Dakota were recently given 122.5 million dollars by a law court. This was in return for the land of the Black Hills that was taken from them in 1877. Other tribes have also sued the US government for broken treaties of the past. These court cases are a sign of the increased power of the tribes of today.

Earning a living

Some tribes are now making money from their reservations. The Mescalero Apache reservation is sited on some of the highest mountain areas in New Mexico. On this difficult land they run a number of successful businesses. They own a multimillion dollar logging company and cattle ranch and have recently built a luxury ski and leisure resort. Most of the people live in new two-storey houses.

Relying on tourists

While a few tribes have been able to make money, most have remained in a state of poverty. Many rely on the interest in their culture as a tourist attraction to earn a living. Most reservations have tourist shops where such things as traditional Indian rugs and jewellery are sold.

Source A

Inuits hunting on Baffin Island. ◀

Source B ▶

This quartzite statue in Nevada advertises Indian crafts which are bought by tourists.

Source C

In 1986 the United States Information Agency said this about the quality of life for modern Indians:

'In spite of many gains made by the Indians, they still lag far behind most Americans in health, wealth and education. In 1984, the unemployment rate among Indians was 39% — more than five times the national rate. Nearly a quarter of all Indian families live on incomes below the poverty level. Diabetes, pneumonia, influenza and alcoholism claim twice as many Indian lives as other American lives.'

United States Information Agency, 1986

The move to the cities

The conditions on some reservations have resulted in many Indians moving to the cities, where work is not easy to find and housing is expensive. Some have done well in their new city lives, while others have ended up in the slums.

Source D

A young mother watches television with her children in their summer encampment on a Navajo reservation.

Split cultures

Perhaps the greatest problem for Indians today is the feeling of being split between two cultures. Cultural differences can make it difficult for Indians to find employment. Some speak about their feelings of sadness for the culture that has been lost. They cannot live as traditional Indians but they do not really feel a part of modern American culture.

Source E

One of the last old basket weavers from the River Indian Tribes Reservation in Colorado.

Protest and debate

The day-to-day problems for many Indians are great, but they have recently been making their point of view known. An Indian group called the American Indian Movement have, since 1970, drawn attention to Indian issues through protests and political debates. The most dramatic of their protests was in 1973 when they, and Indians from the Pine Ridge Sioux reservation, occupied the village of Wounded Knee, site of the 1890 massacre, for 71 days.

Index

Acknowledgements

Cover: Peter Newark's Western Americana. 4, courtesy of the Southwest Museum, Los Angeles. Photo no. CT.1; 5, Peter Newark's Western Americana, from the original oil in the Buffalo Bill Historical Center, Cody, Wyoming; 6–7t, 21, 22, 30, 32, 33, 41, 43cr, 45tr, 47, 50r, 51, 52, 56, 57, Peter Newark's Western Americana; 6l, Hulton Deutsch Collection; 7r, DPL/ David Phillips; 9 (jewellry), Werner Forman Archive/Field Museum of Natural History, Chicago; 9t, Werner Forman Archive/Plains Indian Museum, Buffalo Bill Historical Center, Cody, Wyoming; 9c, 24–5, 43l, Werner Forman Archive; 9b, Werner Forman Archive/Utah Museum of Natural History, USA; 10–11, 18, by permission of the Trustees of the British Museum; 12–13, Tom Till/©Tony Stone Photolibrary, London; 13B, Werner Forman Archive/Maxwell Museum of Anthropology, New Mexico, USA; 13C, all rights reserved, Photo Archives, Denver Museum of Natural History; 13D, Ancient Art & Architecture Collection; 13E, Wesley Bradfield, courtesy Museum of New Mexico, neg. no. 90278; 14, courtesy of National Museum of the American Indian/Smithsonian Institution, no. 25375; 15, thanks to James C. Laray, United States Park Ranger, Ocmulgee National Monument, Macon, Georgia; 21tr, 43tr, Werner Forman Archive/Museum für Völkerkunde, Berlin; 21(Seattle's speech), courtesy of Herbert Johnson Museum of Art, Cornell University; 24b, 31, Denver Art Museum; 25t, George Catlin: Pipestone Quarry, 1830s, oil, Reg. No. 01762168, from the Collection of Gilcrease Museum, Tulsa, Oklahoma; 27, Archiv für Kunst und Geschichte, Berlin/ Montana Historical Society; 34, Werner Forman Archive/The Bradford Collection; 35, National Anthropological Archives, Smithsonian Institution; 38l, Charles Russell: The Storyteller, 1880s, watercolour on paperboard, Reg. No. 0237-1410. From the Collection of Gilcrease Museum, Tulsa, Oklahoma; 38–9, South Dakota State Historical Society, Pierre; 37, Werner Forman Archive/ Brown Museum, Providence, Rhode Island, USA; 42, ©Musée de l'Homme, Paris/J. Oster; 43bl, Werner Forman Archive/P.C. Holland; 43br, Telegraph Colour Library; 45tl, 49br, Werner Forman Archive/British Museum, London; 45b, Library of Congress; 46, Archiv für Kunst und Geschichte, Berlin/Private Collection, Chicago; 48, Minnesota Historical Society/photo: Adrian J. Ebell, Whitneys Gallery, St Paul; 49tl, Minnesota Historical Society; 53b, Nebraska State Historical Society; 55t, 55 (chipped points), Werner Forman Archive/Robert H. Lowie Museum of Anthropology, University of California, Berkeley; 55c, Michael MacIntyre/The Hutchison Library; 55b, Patsy Davidson/Topham Picture Library; 60–1 (background), 60r, 61r, Christine Osborne; 60l, Disappearing World/The Hutchison Library; 61l, Pern/The Hutchison Library